DAY TRADING OPTIONS BEGINNERS GUIDE:

THE CRASH COURSE PLAYBOOK TO THE STOCK MARKET. LEARN HOW TO MAKE MONEY TO CREATE A PASSIVE INCOME INVESTING AND TRADE FOR A LIVING WITH SUCCESSFUL STRATEGIES.

I0510388

BRANDON BLUEPRINTS

Copyright © 2019 by Brandon Blueprints.

All rights reserved. No part of this book may be used or reproduced in any manner whatsoever without written permission except in the case of brief quotations embodied in critical articles or reviews. Although the author and publisher have made every effort to ensure that the information in this book was correct at press time, the author and publisher do not assume and hereby disclaim any liability to any party for any loss, damage or disruption caused by errors or omissions, whether such errors or omissions result from negligence, accident, or any other cause.

DISCLAIMER

The information contained in this book is for general information and educational purposes only.
This book assumes no responsibility for errors or omissions in the contents of the service.
This book has no liability for any damage or loss (including, without limitation, financial loss of profits, loss of business or any indirect or consequential loss).

Table Of Contents

Description

Trading in the stock market can be a cutthroat experience and nowhere is it more cutthroat than in the world of day trading. As such, it is especially important to you continue to learn all you can and develop a ravenous need for new strategies because you can be sure that that is what your competition is doing.

Just because you are day trading, however, doesn't mean that you need to focus on constantly trading all of the time. The fact of the matter is that some days, and even some weeks, the market simply isn't going to want to cooperate. Truly successful traders learn to make the most of the good trades that come their way and not to force it on the days that absolutely nothing is happening. Forcing a trade where none exists is only going to cause you anxiety, frustration, cost you capital for trade fees and hurt your trade percentage to boot. Take advantage of the time off to clear your head and come back ready for success when the market is more agreeable. Focus on quality over quantity and you are far more likely to find the success you seek. Remember, day trading successfully is a marathon, not a sprint, slow and steady wins the race.

Options are tightly connected to stocks, but you can have options for futures, forex, or any other financial instrument. If you are a beginning, start out with equity options. If you already trade forex or futures, you can start with those. Either way, options are a good way to make money while simultaneously limiting risk.

This guide will focus on the following:

- Covered Calls
- Picking Out Some Good Strategies to Use with Options Trading
- Technical Indicators
- Technical Analysis
- Options Greeks
- Trading the SPX and SPY
- Strategic Planning for Options Trading
- Basic Options Trading Strategies
- Learning How to Read an Options Chart
- Options Trading Q & A
- Options on Other Instruments
- The Basic Butterfly Spread Strategy
- How to Keep a Day Trading Journal and Why It's Important
- Price Action Patterns
- Tailoring Binary Options
- Mistakes to Avoid... AND MORE!!!

Introduction

Day trading options is an incredible way to leverage a less risky market to increase your profitability and earn yourself a passive income stream. It is no secret that one of the most profitable passive income streams is the stock market itself, yet the open stock market can be risky and hard to trade, especially if you want to limit your time that you spend actively trading. If you want to earn the increased profit of day trading while also taking advantage of the decreased risks of options, day trading options is the best opportunity for you to go forward with.

By now you should feel confident that you can earn a strong passive income through day trading options, so long as you follow the strategies given to you in this book. Through following all of the steps here, as outlined in the anatomy of trade and using the advice I have given you, you have everything that you need to succeed. All that is left to do is for you to go ahead and get started so that you can begin earning a profit!

As you go forward, I urge you to keep this book nearby as you will find that it serves as an excellent guide in helping you stay on track with your success and increasing your skill over time. This book has plenty of great strategies for you to execute, as well as guidance on how you can structure your plans for turning this into a passive income and for increasing profits. Although there is always something new to learn, a large part of experiencing success in any form of trade is sticking to what you know and following the same strategies over and over again. In doing so, you increase your confidence in your skill and make it easier for you to succeed.

Options can be used to generate profit or as insurance. The insurance fee is generally considered the premium paid. Premiums are based off time to expiration, volatility, and the difference between the spot and strike prices, also known as the intrinsic value. OTM are the cheapest, ATM are the in the middle, and ITM are the most expensive. This is due to intrinsic value. There are two styles of options, American and European, that have different rules governing when one can exercise them.

There are two types of options, calls and puts, and they can be mixed for various strategies.

Everything in this book can be used or modified. The most basic strategies are widely applied, and you, as the investor, should modify them to fit your trading strategies and techniques. If you like a lot of risk and are willing to take it for small profits, you may be interested in writing options. If you just want to have a little insurance, go with simple hedging strategies. If you want to speculate, options are a good way to do it without losing a lot of money. You can also leverage yourself, because you can buy the right to 10,000 shares but only pay the premium – you don't have to outlay cash for all 10,000 shares. Even when you execute, you can borrow from your broker since you will turn around and sell the shares straight back to the market.

Chapter 1 - Covered Calls

A Covered Call is a strategy used to increase the yield on a stock (or generate a yield for a non-dividend stock) and/or to provide a limited (downside) hedge to one's stock position – this dual+ benefit makes this a popular strategy for stock investors.

A Covered Call is a very simple strategy that is comprised of long stock and a sold Call (obviously of the same underlying). For example, assume you are the owner of 1,000 shares of stock ABC (you purchased at $47). Using the data in ABC's Option Chain in Exhibit 4.1, a Covered Call would be structured as follows:

Currently own 1,000 shares ABC stock @ $47 per share

= Sell (10) ABC JAN 47.0 Strike Calls for 1.41

= (10) x 1.41 x 100

= $(1,410) *Total Proceeds* (less commissions)

In this example you sold the JAN 47.0 strike Calls against your long ABC stock position (thus creating a Covered Call) – your Call sale generated proceeds of ($1,410) against your long stock position of $47,000 (= 1,000 shares x $47) thus your potential yield over the holding period (i.e. until the JAN Expiration) is 3% (= $1,410 / $47,000). This yield will only be realized if ABC shares trade above $47 by Expiration – if not, the Covered Call has the dual benefit of protecting losses on the shares to an amount equal to the share price less the premium from the sold Calls, thus for this example, losses on ABC share decline would be hedged to \$45.59 (= \$47 − 1.41). The Covered Call thus enabled you to generate some yield on the shares while simultaneously providing a limited hedge from potential adverse declines in the stock. Nice!

Exhibit 4.1: Option Chain for ABC Stock

Stock: ABC @ \$47.00
Today: December 2
SERIES: JANUARY

CALLS					PUTS			

BID	ASK	Volume	O.I.	STRIKE	BID	ASK	Volume	O.I.
2.68	2.70	41	8,063	JAN 45.0	0.69	0.70	24	5,016
1.99	2.01	19	6,223	JAN 46.0	1.00	1.01	43	684
1.41	1.43	109	3,655	JAN 47.0	1.41	1.44	57	400
0.96	0.97	111	4,174	JAN 48.0	1.96	1.98	51	403
0.63	0.64	44	301	JAN 49.0	2.63	2.65	0	417

SELECTION

Overview

There are many factors and considerations that go into selecting "the best" Covered Call structure. How does one choose the best Call Strike and Expiration to use? Although the best choice will only be known at some point in the future (when the options expire), generally the most logical approach to determine which Strike and Expiration to use is to first ask what is the primary purpose of the strategy? I discuss each below.

Hedge

If the primary purpose is to hedge an existing stock position several interrelated factors need to be considered to choose the optimal Strike and Expiration. First, you need to determine how much "hedge" you think you need and over what time period you need it – basically how much premium do you need to sell in order to cover expected (potential) losses over the chosen time period? At the same time you need to know at what price you are fine with having your shares called away if the stock doesn't drop but instead increases in price. Answers to these two questions *may* determine the best Strike and Expiration to use – in some cases neither of your criteria will be fulfilled, and in such a situation perhaps it is time to consider alternative strategies.

Let's look at how this works. Using the data in Exhibit 4.1 assume you own ABC shares at $45 and they now trade at $47. You are not bearish on the shares but feel they could potentially sell off $1 over the near term – also, given that you purchased them at $45, you don't mind having the shares called away (i.e. selling the shares) above $47. Thus ideally you want $1 of downside protection from the $47 price level over the near term (in this example, the January expiration). Checking the JAN Option Chains, you find that the JAN 47.0 Strike Calls are able to be sold (the Bid price) at 1.41, thus exceeding your requirement for $1.00 of downside protection – you, however, also see that the 48.0 Strike can be sold for 0.96 or basically $1 (close enough). For you the 48.0 Strike is the best choice: not only do you get roughly $1 in downside protection but you also get the possibility to have more upside if the shares continue to rally – as such, instead of getting called away at $47, you get called away $1 higher or at $48. Finding the optimal Strike/Expiration is an iterative process.

Generate or Enhance Yield

The other primary use of the Covered Call strategy is to generate yield (for stocks without dividends) or to enhance yield (for stocks with dividends). Finding the best structure when using Covered Calls for yield purposes is determined, again, by deciding how much yield you want over a given time period and at what price you are willing to have the shares called away. For example, let's say you are seeking yield opportunities and want to hold the position for around six months. You like QRS stock: although it doesn't pay a dividend the stock has been slowly trending up the past year (which you expect to continue) and the company possesses strong fundamentals that match your conservative style of investing and allay your fears an aggressive downside move in the stock. Your goal, however, is to seek maximum yield over the next six months. You check the QRS DEC Option Chains and find the following prices:

Option Chain for QRS Stock

Stock: QRS @ $37.12
Today: June 7
SERIES: DECEMBER

CALLS					PUTS			

BID	ASK	Volume	O.I.	STRIKE	BID	ASK	Volume	O.I.
4.90	5.00	58	337	DEC 36.0	4.25	4.35	56	1,616
4.35	4.45	180	161	DEC 37.0	4.70	4.80	173	1,254
3.85	3.95	160	229	DEC 38.0	5.20	5.30	160	1,657

3.40	3.50	276	551	DE C 39.0	5.75	5.85	39	2,310
2.98	3.05	103	3,016	DE C 40.0	6.30	6.40	15	3,492

A good way to determine the best choice is to simply calculate the (approximate) six-month yields for selling premium from Strikes 37.0 to 40.0 against buying stock at $37.12 – this is how you do it:

37.0 Strike Yield = 4.35 - $0.12 = 4.23 / $37.12 = 11.4%

38.0 Strike Yield = 3.85 / $37.12 = 10.4%

39.0 Strike Yield = 3.40 / $37.12 = 9.2%

40.0 Strike Yield = 2.98 / $37.12 = 8.0%

From the data calculated above, the highest yielding choice is to sell the 37.0 Strike Call premium against the shares – note the need to deduct the amount the share price is above the Strike price from the premium of the 37.0 Strike Calls (basically you purchased the shares at $37.12 but they'll be called away at 37.0 if in-the-money at expiration so the excess $0.12 represents intrinsic value of which you won't get!). Although this may be the highest yielding choice, it doesn't represent the highest Total Return choice. Total Return basically factors in the total premium sold and the appreciation (if any) of the share price – a Total Return calculation assumes the shares trade above the sold Call Strike by expiration. Let's calculate the Total Return (TR) for the previous choices:

37.0 Strike TR = [(37.0 - \$37.12) + 4.35] / \$37.12 = 11.4%

38.0 Strike TR = [(38.0 - \$37.12) + 3.85] / \$37.12 = 12.7%

39.0 Strike TR = [(39.0 - \$37.12) + 3.40] / \$37.12 = 14.2%

40.0 Strike TR = [(40.0 - \$37.12) + 2.98] / \$37.12 = 15.8%

Although the higher Strike Calls (the 40.0 Strike) produce the highest Total Return, this is a lower probability scenario given the shares need to actually trade there to realize that return. Despite this fact, the exercise provides a useful function within the context of this particular example: i.e. QRS shares are trending upwards. The question to ponder then is where you think the shares will trade by DEC expiration? Do you take the potential robust 11.4% yield offered by the 37.0 Strike or do you think the shares will continue to rise and thus sell a higher Strike for even more return? Only you can decide the best choice. As with the hedge example, again determining the best Strike and Expiration is an iterative process.

Important! Cost Basis & Holding Period

It is important to be aware of the cost basis and associated holding period of your shares prior to executing a Covered Call strategy (i.e. at what price did you buy the shares and when did you buy them?) – these are factors which may or may not have important tax implications (this is very specific to each investor's situation and therefore outside of the scope of this book). Basically, whatever Strike you sell (against your shares) will determine the price your shares will be "called away" if the share price trades above the Strike by Expiration – being "called away" is the same as selling the shares. For example, if you purchased XYZ shares at $30 (your "cost basis") and you sold the 36.0 Strike Calls against, your shares will be called away if (and only if) XYZ is trading above $36 by the Expiration date of the Calls. Note that if you sell a Strike that is *below* your cost basis on the shares (and you hold the position until Expiration) your shares will be called away at the Strike price and you will take a loss on the shares. For example assume you purchased the XYZ shares at $36.50 and you decided to sell the 36.0 Strike Calls against (not an uncommon strategy). If XYZ shares trade above $36 by Expiration and you hold the position your shares will be called away at $36 – if you owned 1,000 shares you would thus incur a $500 loss (= (1,000 x $36.5) – 36,000). It is also important to be aware of is how long you have owned the shares, i.e. a few days or a few years – again if the shares trade above the sold Call Strike by expiration, your shares will sold at that Strike price and may produce a taxable event unique to your own situation (i.e. a long or short term capital gain and associated taxes, for example. Be aware of the implications of using this strategy – consult your tax advisor if necessary!

ENTRY EXECUTION

Executing a Covered Call is a relatively straightforward process. The goal of a Covered Call entry execution (actually all entries) is to enter at little to no slippage – that is, we want to minimize *the cost of execution.* The Bid/Ask on shares is usually around $0.01 – that is the minimum spread so there is nothing you can do about it. The Bid/Ask on the Calls (or any option including Puts), however, is where one needs to take care when executing the trade – attention to this detail can literally save you hundreds if not thousands of dollars over time.

Let's assume you want to do a Covered Call on QRS stock (you currently have no position). You choose the DEC 38.0 Strike Calls and you want to sell them against a QRS stock position of 1,000 shares (and therefore you would sell 10 contracts, or 1,000 / 100). Here are the current market prices (see Exhibit 4.3 for QRS option quotes):

QRS @ $37.11 Bid / $37.12 Ask

QRS DEC 38.0 Strike Call @ 3.85 Bid / 3.95 Ask

If you trade into the position *at the market* price you will take the maximum slippage "hit" of $55 for a 1,000 share and 10 option contract position size (excluding commissions):

Trade	Trade Value	Broker Mark	Difference
Buy 1,000 @ $37.12	$37,120	$37,115	$(5)
Sell (10) @ 3.85	$(3,850)	$(3,900)	$(50)
Total	$33,270	$33,215	$(55)

Although an immediate $55 loss is not that big of a deal (within the context of the trade size) the loss in fact can be avoided entirely or substantially reduced – why pay extra when you don't have too? Also, some options on less liquid stock have very wide Bid / Ask spreads than can be quite costly if not properly handled. For example what if the Bid / Ask spread in our example was 3.50 / 4.30? If you sold the Calls for 3.50 in this situation the broker mark would result in an immediate $400 loss after the trade was executed! In these situations it is usually better to avoid using options.

Returning to the QRS example, we will just have to accept the $5 slippage for the stock leg of this strategy – we can't get a better price with a Bid / Ask spread of $0.01. The focus on the trade entry will thus be with the Calls. First of all, one should only use Limit Orders when executing an option trade (any and all option trades) – this is extremely important. Using Market Orders with options is basically an open invitation to be completely ripped-off / robbed. A Market Order for our current example is likely to result in a fill price of 3.75 (instead of 3.85) even though the current market is showing a Bid / Ask of 3.85 / 3.95 thus handing you an immediate loss of $150 after the trade – this unpunished chicanery happens everyday in the option markets – don't let it happen to you. Limit Orders guard against this happening so make sure to only use these types of orders.

In order to properly execute a Covered Call always use the mid-point of the Bid / Ask spread on the Calls as your opening offer. For example, returning to the QRS entry we would do the following with our broker order:

Buy 1,000 QRS shares at $37.12 = $37,120

Sell 10 QRS DEC 38.0 Strike Calls @ 3.90 = $(3,900)

Net Debit = $33,220

If this is filled the maximum slippage (assuming the option price stays the same immediately after the trade) on this Covered Call entry will be the $5 from the stock leg – note there will be no slippage (i.e. zero cost entry!) from the option leg given they were sold at the exact Bid / Ask mid-point. If this price doesn't fill after a minute or so, reduce the offer in 0.01 increments until filled. Thus for the QRS trade, if we can't fill at the 3.90 level (thus total trade net of $33,220) we would reduce to 3.89 (or increase total trade net of $33,230) and repeat until filled – being aggressive on trade entry using this tactic will likely give you a better price entry 95% of the time.

POSITION MANAGEMENT

It is fairly easy to manage an open Covered Call position. The standard procedure is to basically do nothing – simply leave the position alone. Thus if the stock traded above that price (the Call Strike) by expiration your shares would be called away automatically. If not, you would keep both your shares and the premium you sold from the now worthless Calls. There are, however, two primary circumstances when you may need to actively manage (i.e. close the position or make some other adjustment) the open Covered Call position.

Sell-Off Scenario

The first circumstance is when the stock experiences an immediate or sustained sell-off. Although you have some protection against losses already built into the position (the premium from the sold Calls) what happens or what do you do if the shares sell-off below that level when you are in a Covered Call? The decision is not as easy as it first seems – the available choices from the perspective of the Covered Call are to either hold the position as is, close out the entire position (i.e. sell the shares, Buy-to-Close the Calls) or sell the shares but keep the Calls. Several issues need to be considered and understood for each possibility.

If the decision is to hold the position as is, you simply do nothing: hold the shares and allow the Calls to expire worthless – your loss will simply equal the loss on the shares less the sold Call premium (assuming the shares don't rebound above break-even by expiration, in such case there would be no loss).

If the decision is to close out the entire position your loss would equal the loss on the shares less the gain on the sold Calls – note under this route you will not benefit from the full sold Call premium as you would be buying them back at some amount greater than $0 before expiration. For example, say you had an open Covered Call on stock JKL – you purchased 1,000 shares at $30 and sold 10 of the 31.0 Strike Calls against for 2.00 or $2,000 total proceeds (= 2.00 x (10) x 100). A month prior to expiration the shares drop $4 due to a bad earnings announcement. You lose $4,000 on the shares but luckily the

Calls offset $1,500 of this loss (the Calls are now worth 0.50 per contract) thus on a net basis you lose $2,500. You decide to close out the entire position by selling the shares and buying back the sold Calls for the net loss of $2,500. Note that when you established the position you assumed the sold Calls would offset $2,000 in total potential losses – however, and because you closed out the position early (before Expiration) you only got $1,500 of that value given that the Calls in this example are still worth 0.50! This unexpected outcome always catches those new to Covered Calls off guard – be aware of this issue prior to going into any Covered Call position.

Finally, if the decision is to sell the shares (at a loss) and keep the sold Calls open, extreme care needs to be taken and the risk needs to be understood. This action basically transforms the original conservative long position into a short share, potentially (very) risky position. The typical thought process involved with an investor taking this action is the desire to capture the total premium of the sold Call in order to minimize the loss already taken on the shares – don't fall into this trap. For example, assume that instead of closing out the entire position as you did above with your JKL stock, you instead only sold the stock and kept open the 10 31.0 Strike Calls (you can't stand the thought of "losing" that extra $500 in premium!). As a result of this decision, you are now effectively *short* 1,000 shares of JKL at $31. What happens if a positive news item causes the shares to spike for example $3 or more? If this happens you are likely to give back more (possibly substantially more) than the original $2,000 in premium sold and be forced to close out the Calls in an unfavorable market (high slippage). Although this is likely a low probability scenario, these outcomes do indeed tend to happen when you are most exposed – for this simple reason this route is not recommended!

Chapter 2 - Picking Out Some Good Strategies to Use with Options Trading

One of the first things that you will need to do once you decide to enter the market is pick out a good strategy to use. This strategy is so important because it helps you to know when to enter the market, what to look for in the market, and even when you should leave the market. When it comes to options trading, there are actually quite a few strategies that you can choose to work with. Some of the best choices in strategies include:

Working with a fundamental analysis

The first strategy we are going to take a look at is the fundamental analysis. This is a method that doesn't spend so much time looking at the charts as some of the others. Instead, the trader who uses this is trying to find an underlying asset that they believe to be undervalued at the time, for some reason or another. They hope that once they find it, they will be able to do a fundamental analysis to determine whether the price of this security is going to go up.

There are many things that you need to look at when it comes to a fundamental analysis. Understanding why the asset is undervalued is important as well. As a fundamental analyst, you will take a look at the debt ratio the company has, how long it has been in business, whether it has seen an increase in profits over the past five years, whether it is growing, who manages the business, and so on. The hope is to find an asset that is undervalued, and then purchase it before public opinion changes and the price goes up.

This one can help you to find some securities early while they are still at a discount price. But there is a catch. Many times the price of the security is there for a reason and some of the lower ones are there because they are seen as junk or because the company wasn't able to manage their debts very well. You have to be careful when utilizing this kind of strategy to make sure that it will actually work for you.

The fundamental analysis can take some time to learn how to work with. There are a lot of different factors that you need to work with. You aren't just looking through the charts of a stock or security and where it has gone in the past, even though this is important as well. But you also have to look more at the basics of the company and see how it is doing.

For example, with a fundamental analysis, you need to be able to look at the company and see how its management is doing.

If there are any big changes in the management, then you have to look and see how this is going to shake up the industry and how investors are going to respond. If the change is because one of the board members just decided to retire, it isn't a big deal. But if there were some scandals and other issues and that caused the change in the management, then this can be really difficult to work with and may show that the stock isn't going to go up soon.

You should also look at the debt to income ratio of the company. If the company is taking on too much debt, it means that they won't be able to pay their shareholders, and the value may go down. But the reason of the debt accumulation can matter. If the company did a recent expansion, or purchased some expensive equipment to help them grow, then this is a good thing and the price of the stock should go up shortly.

But, it can also go the other way. If the company took on too much debt because of mismanagement or they just can't seem to make enough to pay down regular debts and the paychecks to their employees, this is going to show poorly on the company. If this is what you are seeing with the company, then it may be time to switch and look for some other securities to work with.

These are just two of the main points that you are going to need to look into when you want to do a fundamental analysis with options. It is a method that a lot of people like to use, but often it is going to be done at the same time as the fundamental analysis, rather than doing it on its own. Many traders like the fundamental analysis because it helps them to find an underlying security that is doing poorly but should turn around soon, but they still like to have some of the technical analysis in place to help them see more about the security.

Tip 12: Working with a technical analysis

For most of the strategies we will explore, you will employ a technical analysis. The technical analysis can be a great option because it relies on research of the charts and the history of a particular option. It assumes that all of the other information about the company, including its work, public perception, and anything else explored in a fundamental analysis, is already accounted for in the price.

This can make things a bit easier for you. You get the benefit of just looking at the charts for that underlying asset to make your decisions. You can look at how it has behaved in the past, and bring in current news events to see if it is likely the asset will continue on with its current trajectory or move a different way. From this information, you an pick out the right technical analysis strategy and then enter the market when you are ready.

Before using this strategy, make sure that you are ready and you fully understand the way that it should work. Have lots of charts to back you up, and some good news sources so you can pay attention to anything that may affect the current market for the options you are in.

A technical analysis is going to be a type of trading strategy that is going to evaluate the investments and then identify the trading opportunities that come with that.

Unlike what we saw with the fundamental analysis, or those who like to look at the intrinsic value of the company, a technical analyst is going to focus on some of the patterns that come with price movements, trading signals, and other charting tools to help evaluate how weak or strong the security is at that particular time.

You are able to work with a technical analysis on any kind of security, as long as it has a historical type of trading data that you can look through. This means that you are able to use it with any security such as stocks, commodities, fixed income, currencies, futures, and other types of securities. All of the different strategies that we are going to talk about below will work on the idea of a technical analysis as well, which means that there are plenty of opportunities for you to utilize the tools with this method.

The technical analysis can be a really great way for you to invest and see some great results. Some of the different key takeaways that you can consider when it comes to a technical analysis includes:

1. This kind of strategy is going to ask the trader to evaluate the different investments they want to work with and then identify some of the best trading opportunities in price trends and various patterns that are found on the charts.

2. The analysts and traders who use this method believe that the past activity of that security, and any price changes that occur with that security, can be

valuable because they indicate the price movements that security is going to see in the future.

3. A technical analysis is often going to be contrasted against a fundamental analysis. Sometimes the two of these are used together to really help the trader figure out the right securities to trade in order to get a goo deal on the security, and to figure out which direction it is going to take in the future.

Strategies in a bullish market

Bullish strategies are going to be employed when an options trader expects that the stock price is going to move up. They can also use time decay in a comb of bulls and bears, which is known as a Calendar Spread, and not even need to rely on the movement of the stock. You also have the option of just assessing how high the price of the stock can reasonably go in a certain time frame and then optimize this by purchasing a bullish option. But with most bullish trading strategies, the trader would simply use the idea of purchasing a call option.

Chapter 3 - Options Trading Lingo

In order to effectively operate in the options market, you will need to be familiar with numerous key phrases.

Strike Price: Is defined as the amount at which the stock underlying the option can ultimately be either sold or purchased for based on the agreement in the option.

Exercised: When the holder determines that the agreement in a specific option is in their best interest and decides to put it into action then that option is said to be exercised.

Trading out: While options can be either exercised or not, they can also be traded out. Also known as closing out, this is when an investor sells an option that could be profitably exercised onto the open market where it is then bought back by the original writer who buys the positions back and closes it. In general, just over 50% of all options are traded out while 10% are actually exercised, and the rest expire worthlessly.

Listed: Options are traded via official and unofficial channels, those that are traded on a national exchange for options are said to be listed. They then have a strike price that is fixed as well as a clearly defined date of expiration. Listed options typically count for 100 shares of any given underlying stock.

In the money: Call options can be considered in the money provided the current underlying stock share is above the strike price at the given moment.

Intrinsic value: When an option is in the money, its intrinsic value is calculated as the difference between its current price and its strike price.

Time value: The amount of time a specific option has left is said to be its remaining time value.

Volatility: The price that an option currently occupies can be either stable or precarious and prone to additional positive or negative movement, an option related to an unstable stock is said to have a higher amount of volatility.

Premium: The complete price of a specific option which is a combination of volatility, time value, strike price and stock price.

Option functions

Speculation: The two most common reasons that traders buy options is to hedge an existing trade or to speculate on future movement. Options are ideal for speculation purposes as traders can bet that an underlying security is going to move in a specific way with confidence as they can always choose not to exercise their option. This does not mean it is not without risk, however, as you still have to choose correctly when it comes to the direction the underlying asset is going to move in as well as the amount of that movement in order to find success. Nevertheless, options trading remains a popular investment choice as it doesn't take much to start seeing a profit.

Hedging: Hedging, on the other hand, can be considered a type of insurance policy that can help traders ensure that an existing investment is covered when they expect that sector of the market to take a significant hit. Alternately, it can make otherwise risky investments far more manageable as traders can purchase their risky proposition, along with an option for the same amount of the underlying asset at the current price, before moving forward confident that they will at least be able to break even.

Chapter 4 - Technical Indicators

In options trading, technical indicators are used to enable the trader to determine a couple of facts. These include the following:

- Duration of stock movement

- Direction of the move

- Movement range

There is a difference between trading options and other securities. The main differences are that options are subject to time decay and their value diminishes as time goes. The holding period is therefore quite significant. For this reason, the difference between an ordinary trader and an options trader is clearly visible.

An options trader is constrained by time while an ordinary trader can hold a position indefinitely. This is the major difference between the two and hence the need for additional technical indicators.

1. Relative Strength Index

One of the most useful indicators for options traders is the relative strength index. The RSI is a momentum indicator and is used by traders to compare the size of gains made recently to losses incurred over a particular time period. Using the RSI, a trader is able to measure a stock's change in price and speed movement.

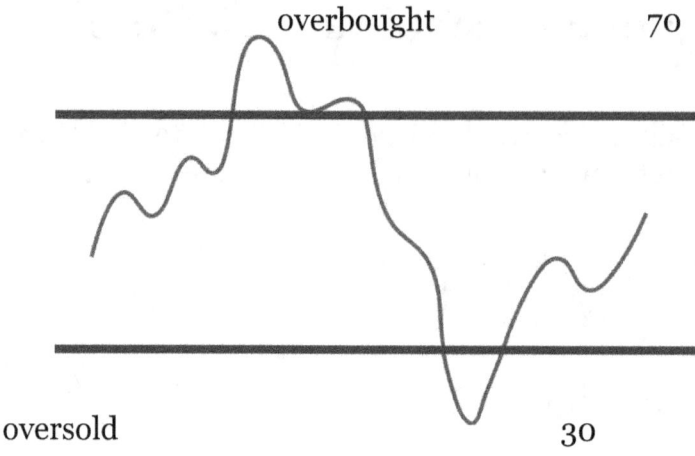

overbought   70

oversold   30

The aim of these parameters is to help a trader determine which stocks or securities have been oversold or overbought. This is usually achieved by using values that range from 0 to 100. Now any values above 70 indicate that the stock has been overbought while values below 30 simply imply that a stock has been oversold.

RSI ideally works best with stocks and options rather than indexes. Stocks tend to clearly indicate their status as either overbought or oversold. This makes it easy for options traders to tell which stocks are oversold, which ones are overbought, and which ones are available. It is not that simple with indexes. The best stocks for options traders are often high-beta stocks that are very liquid especially for short-term trading.

2. Simple Moving Averages

Some of the most important and widely used technical indicators are moving averages. Their main purpose is to smooth out the price pattern and to provide clear indication whether a stock is trending or is within a trading range. The moving averages are basically based on the mean stock price, usually the closing price.

If we take the 20-day moving average, we would consider the mean of the stock's closing price for the past 20 days. This average change each day as long as the particular stock is traded. Therefore, the 20-day Moving Average will have a different value each day. This tends to create a trend of a particular stock that keeps moving.

Charting

Normally, when we chart the price pattern, the resulting chart indicates a very volatile pattern. It is possible for the price to vary by as much as $3 or even $5 in a single day. Now if we take the 20-day moving average to the same chart, then the price pattern will be smoothened out.

The reason why the price is smoothed out is that the Moving Average takes into account the 20 days worth of data. This tends to smooth out the volatile price pattern, making it easier for an options trader to disseminate information.

Summary

Moving averages are crucial technical indicators. They provide information that is of paramount importance to options traders. The averages are based on the average closing price of a stock for a set number of days. When applied to the stock's price chart, they smooth out the price pattern. This makes it easier to note if the stock has an upward or downward trend.

3. Exponential Moving Averages

Apart from the simple moving averages that we have observed, we also have the exponential moving averages. With the simple moving averages, we considered all the 20 days' prices as having the same weight when working out the averages. However, this is not the case when it comes to the exponential moving averages or EMAs.

Due to the weighted prices, the EMA or exponential moving averages tend to respond much faster than the SMA or simple moving averages. The EMA also starts to respond and trend upwards much faster compared to the SMA. As a trader, which one of these two moving averages should you consider? Well, both averages have their own merits. The exponential moving average might register false alarms should they occur. The simple moving average resists false alarms and is also resistant to other challenges.

However, we also note that the EMA or exponential moving average is able to react faster to price volatility in the market. In options trading, traders prefer the EMA over the SMA because they are far more sensitive to price changes and showcase quick movements. The quick and sensitive movements are preferred by options traders especially due to the volatile yet short-term nature of options trading.

Summary

This makes them more sensitive to price fluctuations and can react better to such changes. These are the properties that make them suitable for options trading.

The main aim of the averages is to indicate the direction of a stock. The averages will indicate whether a stock is trending downwards, upwards, or sideways. This kind of information is useful to options traders because they will be able to avoid trading in stock stuck in a trading range or on a downward trend.

Both the simple and exponential moving averages are useful in other ways as well. For instance, if the stock price moves above or below the moving average, we will know that there is a reversal of the current trend and a new trend is probably about to begin. When the stock price crosses the moving averages line from below moving upwards, it shows that investors and traders are beginning to purchase the stock.

As the trend begins to move upwards, it indicates a great opportunity to purchase call options or acquire a bullish option strategy. However, when the stock price crosses the EMA and starts to trend downwards, then this becomes a great opportunity to set up a bearish options strategy.

False Alarms

There can be some challenges with the moving averages, especially the Simple Moving Average or SMA. Apparently, they sometimes give off false alarms. For instance, the stock price crosses the moving average line several times within a couple of months. If a trader had relied on the moving averages to buy stock options, then they would have suffered painful losses.

The reasons for the false alarms are mostly due to the sensitivity of the 20-Day simple moving average. This particular technical indicator is erratic and too sensitive. It is possible, fortunately, to modify these indicators so that they are focused on specific periods of time or even certain date ranges. We can, for instance, work with a 50-day exponential moving average rather than the 20-day SMA.

Chapter 5 - Technical Analysis

When working with technical analysis you are always going to want to remember that it functions because of the belief that the way the price of a given trade has moved in the past is going to be an equally reliable metric for determining what it is likely to do again in the future. Regardless of which market you choose to focus on, you'll find that there is always more technical data available than you will ever be able to realistically parse without quite a significant amount of help. Luckily, you won't be sifting through the data all on your own, and you will have numerous technical tools including things such as charts, trends, and indicators to help you push your success rates to new heights.

While some of the methods you will be asked to apply might seem arcane at first, the fact of the matter is that all you are essentially doing is looking to determine future trends along with their relative strengths. This, in turn, is crucial to your long-term success and will make each of your trades more reliable practically every single time.

Understand core assumptions: Technical analysis is all about measuring the relative value of a particular trade or underlying asset by using available tools to find otherwise invisible patterns that, ideally, few other people have currently noticed. When it comes to using technical analysis properly you are going to always need to assume three things are true. First and foremost, the market ultimately discounts everything; second, trends will always be an adequate predictor of price and third, history is bound to repeat itself when given enough time to do so.

Technical analysis believes that the current price of the underlying asset in question is the only metric that matters when it comes to looking into the current state of things outside of the market, specifically because everything else is already automatically factored in when the current price is set as it is. As such, to accurately use this type of analysis all you need to know is the current price of the potential trade in question as well as the greater economic climate as a whole.

Those who practice technical analysis are then able to interpret what the price is suggesting about market sentiment in order to make predictions about where the price of a given cryptocurrency is going to go in the future. This is possible due to the fact that pricing movements aren't random. Instead, they follow trends that appear in both the short and the long-term. Determining these trends in advance is key to using technical analysis successfully because all trends are likely to repeat themselves over time, thus the use of historical charts in order to determine likely trends in the future.

When it comes to technical analysis, the what, is always going to be more important than the why. That is, the fact that the price moved in a specific way is far more important to a technical analyst then why it made that particular movement. Supply and demand should always be consulted, but beyond that, there are likely too many variables to make it worthwhile to consider all of them as opposed to their results.

Price charts
Technical analysis is all about the price chart which is a chart with an x and y axis. The price is measured along the vertical axis and the time is measured via the horizontal axis. There are numerous different types of price charts that different types of traders prefer, these include the point and figure chart, the Renko chart, the Kagi chart, the Heikin-Ashi chart, the bar chart, the candlestick chart, the line chart, and the tick chart. However, the ones you will need to concern yourself with at first are going to be included in any forex trading platform software and are the bar chart, the candlestick chart, the line chart, and

the point and click chart which is why they are outlined in greater detail below.

Line chart: Of all the various types of charts, the line charts is the simplest because it only presents price information in the form of closing prices in a fixed time span. The lines that give it its name are created when the various closing price points are then connected with a line. When looking at a line chart it is important to keep in mind that they will not be able to provide an accurate visual representation of the range that individual points reached which means you won't be able to see either opening prices or those that were high or low prior to close. Regardless, the closing point is important to always consider which is why this chart is so commonly referred to by technical traders of all skill levels.

Bar chart: A bar chart takes the information that can be found in a line chart and expands upon it in a number of interesting ways. For starters, the chart is made using a number of vertical lines that provide information on various data points. The top and bottom of the line can then be thought of as the high and low of the trading timeframe respectively while the closing price is also indicated with a dash on the right side of the bar. Furthermore, the point where the currency price opened is indicated via a dash and will show up on the left side of the bar in question.

Candlestick chart: A candlestick chart is similar to a bar chart, though the information it provides is much more detailed overall. Like a bar chart it includes a line to indicate the range for the day, however, when you are looking at a candlestick chart you will notice a wide bar near the vertical line which indicates the degree of the difference the price saw throughout the day. If the price that the stock is trading at increases overall for the day, then the candlestick will often be clear while if the price has decreased then the candlestick is going to be read.

Point and figure chart: While seen less frequently than some of the other types of charts, a point and figure chart has been around for nearly a century and can still be useful in certain situations today. This chart can accurately reflect the way price is going to move, though it won't indicate timing or volume. It can be thought of as a pure indicator of price with the excessive noise surrounding the market muted, ensuring nothing is skewed.

A point and figure chart is noticeable because it is made up of Xs and Os rather than lines and points. The Xs will indicate points where positive trends occurred while the Os will indicate periods of downward movement. You will also notice numbers and letters listed along the bottom of the chart which corresponds to months as well as dates. This type of chart will also make it clear how much the price is going to have to move in order for an X to become an O or an O to become an X.

Trend or range: When it comes to using technical analysis successfully, you will want to determine early on if you are more interested in trading based on the trends you find or on the range. While they are both properties related to price, these two concepts are very different in practice which means you will want to choose one to emphasize over the other. If you decide to trade according to trend, then you are more interested in going with the flow and choosing stocks to trade while everyone else is having the same idea.

Chart Patterns to Be Aware Of

Flags and Pennants: Both flags and pennants show retracement, that is deviations that will be visible in the short term in relation to the primary trend. Retracement results in no breakout occurring from either the resistance or support levels but this won't matter as the security will also not be following the dominant trend. The lack of breakout means this trend will be relatively short term. The resistance and support lines of the pennant occur within a larger trend and converge so precisely that they practically form a point. A flag is essentially the same except that the resistance and support lines from the flag will be essentially parallel instead.

If you are looking for them, both flags and pennants are more likely to be found in the mid-section of the primary phase of the trend. They can last up to two weeks before being absorbed back into the primary trend line. They are typically associated with falling volume which means that if you notice a flag or a pennant and the volume is not falling then you are more likely actually seeing a reversal which is an actually changing trend instead of a simple retracement.

Head Above Shoulders Formation: If you are looking for indicators of how long any one particular trend is likely to continue, then looking for a grouping of three peaks in a price chart, known as the head above shoulders formation, can indicate a bearish pattern moving forward. The peaks to the left and to the right of the primary peak, also known as the shoulders, should be somewhat smaller than the head peak and also connect at a specific price. This price is known as the neckline and when it reaches the right shoulder the price will likely then plunge noticeably.

Chapter 6 - Options Greeks

Advanced options traders probably understand the Greeks. They say that trading options but without knowledge of the Greeks is akin to flying an aircraft without knowing how the instruments work. While you may be okay when everything is going on well, you will definitely crash the plane should something go wrong.

The problem is that most traders won't be bothered to learn about the Greeks or the concepts they represent. This can cause problems later on so it is important to learn a little about them.

What are the Greeks?

The Greeks are delta, gamma, theta, vega, and rho. Understanding the concepts they stand for is of paramount importance. You may ignore, if you like, the mathematical formula. It is much more important to learn about what the numbers mean rather than the complex mathematics associated with them.

One important factor that you need to keep in mind is that the figures assigned to the Greeks are all theoretical. This means that mathematical models are used to arrive at the values. The Greeks have to be calculated and the model used will determine their accuracy.

Greek Matrix

The matrix shown is a Greek matrix. It showcases many different option strikes from the months of March and April of 2018. The stock was trading at $60 then. Our matrix shows delta, gamma, theta, and vega values as well as the mid-market price. The gamma, delta, vega, and theta figures indicated in the matrix above have been formatted for the US dollar. To do this, all that you have to do is use the contract multiplier of the option. This will give you the normalized dollar values.

Delta and Gamma Values

Delta

Delta is used to gauge the sensitivity of the theoretical value of an option based on the price changes of the underlying security. Delta has a value that lies between 1 and -1. The value of delta simply points to the changes in the value of an option when the underlying stock's price changes by a dollar. The value of delta is sometimes represented as a value between 100 and -100. This is done in order to showcase the dollar value

Example

Let us assume that you once owned the January 60 put which had a delta value of -50. This simply means that if the price of the underlying stock went up by a dollar, then you would suffer a loss of $50.

Most advanced options traders are acquainted with Delta. Delta represents options price change together with the corresponding movement of the underlying stock. It is often indicated as a percentage. When stocks trade higher, the Delta value also increases. Now Delta is closely related to another parameter known as Gamma. You need to understand Delta in order to learn about Gamma.

Gamma

Gamma is the second derivative of Gamma and is closely related to Delta. It informs traders how much the Delta value is going to change based on the movement of the underlying stock. Experts define gamma as the delta's rate of change based on the movement of 1 point in the price of the underlying asset.

While it may sound strange and new, gamma is actually a useful indicator. It is a reliable measure of the value of the second derivative as relates to the underlying stock. As an options trader, you will be seeking a delta hedge strategy in order to bring down the gamma value. This has the effect of maintaining a hedge across a wider price range. When gamma is reduced, though, it results in a reduction of alpha as well.

Greeks Used for Understanding Combination Trades

Using Greeks in this manner enables you to quantify the different risks that you may be exposed to. This is advisable because options positions are known to have some varieties of inherent risk exposures. These tend to vary with market movements and time. It is a good idea to ensure that you understand the risks appropriately.

Summary

The Greeks are absolutely useful tools for any options trader. They provide crucial measures on the position of options' risks as well as possible rewards. You need to ensure that you master the basics so that you can then apply them to your strategies and trades. As a trader, you need to know a lot more than the amount of capital that is at risk. Basically, if you wish to have a clear understanding of the chances of a trade making a profit, then you will have to have the capacity to determine the different risks exposure metrics.

Options trade conditions change frequently. With the Greeks, you are able to determine the sensitivity of any of your trades in relation to the passage of time, volatility, and price fluctuations. If you are to take your options trading to the next level, then you will need to understand the Greeks and then combine your Greeks with strong insights on the risk graphs.

Options Trading Success Stories

Vince Stanzione

Vince Stanzione is a successful financial trader, an author, and entrepreneur. He trained to be a trader and started trading the financial markets in 1999. He was successful and made over $3 million working with different firms. By 2003, he had stopped working for major financial firms and set out on his own.

He runs courses today teaching people about spread options trading. He is also an entrepreneur and has managed to set up some very successful companies. Many of them became very successful and went international. In the process, they earned him millions of dollars.

Srirama Tanniru

One of the successful options traders who has been consistent over the years is one Mr. Srirama Tanniru. Mr. Srirama is based in Sacramento, California and is well known for his place in the field of trading and finance.

Mr. Srirama studied computers, information technology, and economics. He went on to love trading and became really good at it. He has worked in many finance company in senior positions.

Today, Mr. Srirama is an accomplished Equity Index options trader, adviser, and risk manager. Not only does he trade frequently, but has also earned top dollar from trading. He also makes money providing professional financial services to clients across California and around the world.

Chapter 7 - Trading the SPX and SPY

An introduction to the SPX

The S&P 500 is an index of the US stock market. This index consists of the stocks or shares of 500 top American companies with Large-Cap. The S&P 500 stock market index belongs to Standard & Poor's, abbreviated as S&P. Standard and Poor's is a division of the giant McGraw-Hill company.

Basically, all the stocks in the S&P index are traded on the two largest stock markets in the USA. These are the New York Stock Exchange and the NASDAQ. The most widely tracked indices of US stocks are the Dow Jones Industrial Average and the S&P 500. The S&P 500 ratio to as the SPX or INX.

There are plenty of exchange-traded funds and index funds that regularly track the daily performance of the SPX or S&P 500. These funds hold stocks similar to those held by this index in the same proportions. The aim is to match its performance on the stock market but before expenses and fees.

These funds choose to align their investment plans with the SPX index because any corporation that has its stock added to the list is likely to perform better at the bourse. The principal will in return boost the performance of the fund as fund managers will most likely buy the shares of companies that get onto the list. The S&P 500 is also used often as a baseline level where the performance of mutual funds and asset management companies is gauged.

Trading the S&P index with leverage

There are various ways of trading options with the S&P 500 index or the SPX. You can trade the SPX Index with some built-in leverage in various ways. These are listed below.

• Trading the SPX Index option itself: with this option, you have zero leverage. This particular trade with the SPX index is not too common because the index is very large and the options are very costly. The bid ask spread is also very wide.

• SPY ETF or Great ETF: With this type, the index here is .01 the size of the SPX. There is excellent liquidity with a $0.01 spread. Here, there is no leverage too and you need to buy huge amounts of shares.

• SSO and SDS: Here you get double the leverage of the SPY which is great. This option provides you with great liquidity which is also another attractive feature. And with a $0.05 bid-ask spread, it is definitely an acceptable option.

Chapter 8 - Strategic Planning for Options Trading

Strategic planning is an integral part of sustainable success, be it in business or in options trading. Let's talk about how to make a game plan for your trades in this chapter.

What is Strategic Planning

The basic ingredients of all these strategies are the two primary options namely the call and put options. The multitude of strategies that are so formulated are the different permutations and combinations of these two and other things.

CBOE- Chicago Board of Options Exchange is the largest such exchange in the world, which offers options on a wide variety of single stocks, indexes, and ETFs. Traders can create multiple option strategies varying from buying or selling a single option to very complex and intricate ones that include multiple simultaneous option positions.

Benefits it Offers

To prevent your emotions from affecting the trade, a plan needs to be created. Experiencing the otherworldly happiness of making a huge gain or a heartbreaking amount of loss can make your mind spin, and you might deviate from the original strategy you had in mind if you had one, which you need to. Strategic planning helps you with that. It gives you detailed yet simplified instructions on specifically how to tackle every trading situation, should they arise. If you are following a well-formed strategy efficiently, you can even handle multiple trades. Thus, you don't need to skip a good opportunity if presented with it. However, taking up too many trades may expose you to too much risk. A well-structured trading strategy tells you both how you are making trades and the reason for which you're doing it.

Not only that, but good strategic planning also guides you on how to monitor the results. One should know whether the strategy they're applying is working in the desired manner. Random trades where one just sells and buys for any reason which seems good, does not give any useful feedback, because the gains and losses will be as random as the impulses which made the trade. But by using strategic planning, the right amount calibrated adjustments can be made to the trading process to improve it overall.

It allows you to be proactive

When you have a plan, you can predict the future better and prepare accordingly. It helps you anticipate unfavorable scenarios and take the necessary actions to avoid negative impacts. This way, you are not just reacting to negative situations but are rather proactively avoiding them. Market trends are ever-changing, and if you want to stay on top of your game, you need always to be proactive to stay ahead of the competition.

It gives you a sense of direction

With a strategic plan, you get a bearing of where you currently stand and in what direction you need to go in order to achieve your goals and objectives. When your plan is in sync with your vision and goals, you go forward with that much energy. It also helps you make more efficient decisions and evaluate your success better.

Tips to Develop a Strategic Plan

Now that we've established the need for a strategic plan, we need to know about certain things to develop a strategic plan. Developing a strategic plan takes into consideration a lot of factors.

- *The amount of capital you have*
- *The type of capital you have*
- *Your inclination towards being a bull or a bear*
- *The existing conditions in the market*
- *Market volatility*
- *Technical environment*
- *Your affinity with risk*
- *Are you a long term or short-term investor?*
- *Your technical knowledge and expertise*

Now, this list is not exhaustive but covers a major chunk of all the things you need to take into consideration while developing a strategic plan. Coming to the tips to develop a strategic plan, just know that options are not like any other investments. They require deep analysis and detailed, methodical approaches. So, the first tip would be to see how much capital you have and then choose a strategic plan, which will work efficiently with the amount of capital you have. If you do not have a lot of capital, start with a short-term strategy, which generates profits early so you can gather some more capital and prepare yourself for a more intensive investment. However, with more profit potential comes more risk, and that's where your risk preference comes in. If you're a safe player who wants a stable income even though the rate is lower, then plan a strategy that gives you low but regular returns. If you're a risk taker, then you can aim for greater profits, but take note that you should ideally not invest in higher risk strategies with borrowed capital because the overall liability might increase. Invest in such strategies with your own money and profits, which do not have any inherent liabilities. Another tip would be to determine the direction you want to go with, whether it's going to be a bearish approach or bullish approach. But at the same time, another auxiliary tip would be, to be flexible with your approach. If your general trading style is inclined to the bearish side, but it's reasonably apparent that being a bull about now would be better, and vice versa, then being rigid is not good.

Step-by-step Entry Guide

Before you start making any trades, there are certain things you should check. This is a strategic step-by-step guide that will help you pick great trades and filter out bad trades consistently.

The order facilitates quickly figuring out whether a trade is worth your time.

Portfolio Balance

Portfolio balance is everything. So even before you begin looking for a new trade, you need to ask yourself how it will fit in your portfolio. You need to question whether you need the trade. If, for example, you already have a lot of bullish trades in your portfolio, you probably don't need another one.

Balancing out trades is the key to developing a good portfolio as it reduces risk. So, when you already have a handful of bullish trades, you should be looking for some bearish trades that will offset your risk. When you know what kind of trade you need to look for from the get-go, it helps you filter better and focus only on what your portfolio needs.

Liquidity

Liquidity is one of the most important factors when it comes to picking great, tradable stocks. An illiquid option is not worth your time. So, when looking for a new trade, you should follow this general rule of thumb: if the underlying stock trades approximately 100k shares daily, then it's good to go. Since it's a big and efficient market, we can be confident in the fact that the calculations will only become more accurate as time passes. For underlying options, if the strikes you are trading have at least 1000 open interest contracts, this is preferable. This makes sure you can get in and out of the market fast as it is liquid enough.

Implied Volatility Percentile

This is measured using IV percentiles. So, for example, if GOOG has IV of 40% but an IV percentile of 80%, this means that over the last year, more than 80% of the time the volatility would be lower than it currently is (40%). This implies that the implied volatility for GOOG is relatively high, meaning you should consider premium-selling strategies.

Similarly, if FB has an IV of 35% but an IV percentile of 30%, it means that over the last year, only 30% of the time the IV was lower than what it is currently (35%). This also implies that there is a 70% chance the IV will increase, so the IV is relatively low for FB and you should prefer to be a net buyer.

Picking a Strategy

When we talk about picking the best strategy, it is more about eliminating than selecting. Once you have a good grasp of how the underlying stock's IV and IV percentile affect the options, you can start eliminating strategies that wouldn't make sense here. For example, in case the option pricing is rich, and IV is high, we can eliminate strategies like calendars, long single options, debit spreads, etc. Then we can go ahead and select the best strategy from the ones left (credit spreads, strangles, iron condors, etc.) depending on our account size and risk tolerance.

Strikes & Month

Once you have selected the right strategy, the next step is to place trades at a probability level you're comfortable with. Say, you're going to be selling credit spreads below the market. You could sell your credit spreads at a strike price that gives you a

70% chance of success or a strike price that gives you a 90% chance of success. Both are high probability trades, but one is clearly more aggressive. You can pick either one if you're sure it fits your goals and your style. You also need to give yourself enough time to make sure the trade can work for you. For high IV strategies, you'd want to place them at 30-60 days out, and for low IV strategies, you'd want to go with 60-90 days. Why? Because the longer timeline boosts your theta value and counters the low volatility.

Position Size

One of the most crucial areas where many traders - even the experienced ones - fail is position sizing. There have been numerous studies that have shown that your risk increases exponentially when trading big positions, and you could easily end up blowing up your whole account. This is why for beginners and intermediates I advise going with a small position at all times. Place all your trades on a sliding scale of 1-5% of your total balance. This is your risk scale.

How do you define risk? Simple, it's the cash or margin you put up to cover a trade. If you were to sell a $1 wide credit put spread for 25 cents, you would need to put up $75 margin to cover it. Now, if your account is worth $10,000, and for each trade, you wish to allocate 2% of your account, the $75 margin is what would be used to base the trade-off. So, you can take $200 of risk (2% of $10,000) divided by $75 per contract. This comes out at 2.66, which means you could sell 2.66 spreads at most.

To be safe, you should always round it down, never up.

Just like chess players need to be thinking a few moves ahead (at least the good ones do), a good trader also needs to be thinking ahead. You should always have a Plan B for when things go wrong, and this should mean more than just being able to shield yourself from a losing trade.

Although that is important, you should also be thinking about scenarios where the stock doesn't move, and you might have to roll it over to the next month. You need to know whether the options even exist for the next contract month. The stock might have earnings coming up soon, or a dividend might be paid out soon.

You need to remember that some trades *will* go wrong, as is the way of the market. If you're constantly asking yourself important questions, your brain stays alert and formulates new plans to adjust if the need arises.

Fundamentals of Options Strategies

Long calls

It is the simplest option strategy to learn about. That does not mean the profit-making is easy. It is a bullish strategy, but one must be right about many things to make it profitable. For that, a trader needs to be right about the direction of the stock price movement and the quantum of it. The time it takes to move must also be correct. Right on all these three elements make the long call strategy profitable. The upside profit potential is unlimited but things like volatility and time erosion work against a long option.

Short Calls

These are not good for newbies in options trading. It is also called a naked call, as it is uncovered. It is quite a risky position because the upside risk here is unlimited and the profit is limited (happens when the stock price drops). Short Call Write is a credit strategy where you get money for putting on the position, which puts the broker at risk if you are not able to cover the position when required.

Long puts

Like a long call trade, a long-put trade is simple to understand. Put strategies are generally harder to make a profit in, but the strategy is a basic component of many complex options strategies. A long-put option is bearish in terms of inclination. With long calls, an investor needs to be right about the direction of stock price movement and the amount of it with the time frame to make a profit. The maximum potential loss on a long-put trade equals the price paid for the option. The profit potential, however, is quite substantial if the stock price drops.

Short puts

The short puts are not as risky as the short calls. But that in no way means that newbies in option trading can easily make profits using this strategy. When a put is sold, a profit/loss situation opposite to that of a long put is created. The profit, when the stock price rises, is limited to the premium received on selling the option. The downside risk keeps rising until the stock's value is zero. The margin requirements of this strategy are high, and thus, significant funds are required.

Selecting your strike price

Options traders often have a hard time determining the strike prices they are going to use. The type of strike price (ATM, OTM, ITM) affects the quantum of the movement of the underlying asset price required to make a profit. Even if the underlying stock remains stagnant, profit can be made by using an appropriate strike price. The bearishness or the bullishness of the investor needs to be matched accordingly.

Bullish options strategies

If an investor is extremely bearish, out of the money long puts or in-the-money short calls should be considered. These require a highly bearish move of an equally high quantum in the underlying stock to become profitable. But if you're not that bearish, ITM long puts or OOTM short calls should be considered. OOTM can result in a profit sometimes, even when there's no price change in the underlying stock.

Bearish options strategies

Most option strategies have a higher profit potential when they need a substantial price movement in the underlying stock, but it's also less likely to make a profit. OOTM short puts and OOTM short calls can make a profit possible even with zero movement in the underlying stock. But they are extremely risky. Using credit spreads is a safer alternative but has less profit potential.

Chapter 9 - Basic Options Trading Strategies

There are plenty of varied trading strategies that can be used to trade options. These range from the very simple trades to the absolute complex and exotic trades. However, regardless of how simple or how complex a trade is, it is essentially based on the basic call and put options.

Options trading can be a complex affair. It is definitely more complex compared to traditional stock trading. Ideally, when buying stocks, you will determine how many shares you want and at what price then you will fill out a form so the broker can process your order. When it comes to options trading, you will need these and a lot more.

We shall first examine the five most basic strategies. These very basic strategies used only one option. Investors refer to them as one-legged strategies. While the strategies may be simple, they are by no means risk-free. They simply provide beginners with some of the best and easy ways to get started trading options.

The Five Basic Options Trading Strategies:
- The long call
- The short put
- The long put
- The married put
- The covered call

1. The Long Call Options Trading Strategy

The long call options strategy refers to the strategy in which you purchase a call option. Buying a call option implies going long. When you go long, you expect the underlying stock's price will rise and you stand to make a profit. Let us look at an example of this strategy.

Example:

We have shares of company ABC trading at $50 per share and a call option with a $50 strike. The cost or premium of this share is $5, and the expiry period is after six months. Our options contract, in this case, is for 100 shares so the total premium cost is $5 * 100 = $500.

Potential Benefits and Downsides

Now you stand to benefit in a major way from this contract. For instance, if you time this call well, then your profits are almost infinite. This is as long as the stock price keeps moving higher. You could easily make profits of $5,000 or more in just a short while. However, the downside is that you stand to lose your premium of $500. This is the maximum loss you stand to lose should share price take a nosedive. Even then, you can still recoup some of these losses if you sell the stock before the expiration date. Therefore, the benefit of using the long call strategy is that your losses are limited, but the upside or profitability is virtually unlimited.

Why Adopt This Strategy?

There are a number of reasons why you may adopt this strategy. First, if you are not too concerned about losing the entire premium, then you are able to leverage your predictions of the stock price rising so that you stand to earn much more than directly owning the stock.

You can use this strategy to limit your risk of owning a stock directly. Owning the stock directly can expose you to potential losses while using this strategy limits your risk of loss. Instead of owning a large number of shares from one company, some traders may prefer this approach.

Also, owning a stock directly requires a lot of financial resources compared to just using an option trading strategy. Remember that owning shares means buying them directly at face value, but trading using stock options only requires payment of a premium.

2. The Long Put Options Trading Strategy

The long put trading strategy is very similar to the long call strategy. The only difference here is that you will be hoping that the stock price declines. Stock prices can rise or fall depending on a number of factors. If your predictions or analysis indicate that a stock price will fall, then your best options strategy is the long put.

As an investor, you will buy a put option and then hope that your predictions are correct. Again, if your predictions are correct, then you stand to gain unlimited profits while your losses will be limited to the cost of setting up the option. This is best demonstrated through an example.

Example:

Let us take company ABC whose stock has a current market value of $50 per share. According to your prediction, or analysis, the share price will fall in the next six months. Based on this, you discover there is a put option at $50 strike price that is currently available at $5 per 100 shares. This option has an expiration period of six months.

*Now the call option charges $5 per 100 shares. If you intend to invest in 100 units of shares, then you will pay a premium of $5 * 100 = $500. Your cost and potential loss will therefore, be limited only to this amount. However, should your predictions come true then you stand to benefit much, much more.*

What Are the Potential Losses or Benefits?

If you invest in a long put option trade, then you stand to benefit should your predictions turn out right. You will benefit the most if the share price falls to zero or $0 per share. When this happens, you stand to make $50 * 100 = $5,000.

Now should the price of the stock rise, you can still sell and recoup some of the funds paid for the premium. This helps minimize your losses. However, the maximum amount of losses that you stand to incur is $500 or the cost of the premium.

Why Use This Strategy?

This specific strategy provides an excellent opportunity to wager against an expected stock decline. Should the stock price decline be significant, then you stand to make much more money than through direct investment in the same stock. This is, therefore, one reason why you would wish to invest in a long put option.

There are traders who would wish to use this strategy in order to limit any possible losses arising from price fluctuations. For instance, if the price of a stock falls drastically, then the losses can be huge for any investor. However, mitigating the losses is possible with a long put option. The option provides a better alternative to short selling as the risk is high as the price of a stock could rise indefinitely.

3. The Short Put Options Trading Strategy

Yet another basic strategy that is commonly used to trade options is the short put. This strategy is basically the opposite of the long put. Remember that with the short put, an investor is betting on the price of a stock rising. With this approach, you will be selling put options which is also known as going short.

This specific strategy is pegged on the chance that the price of a particular stock will either rise or stay level until the expiry of the option. It is expected that with this strategy, the option will expire worthless, and as the seller, you will earn a premium for absolutely free. This strategy, just like the long call strategy, can be set up as a strategy to mitigate a rising stock though there are some significant differences.

Potential Benefits and Downsides
Like with all other strategies, there are potential benefits and downsides to this particular strategy. A long call basically counts on a major rise in stock price, the short put option is a

little more modest, and the payoff is also modest. For instance, the long call has the capacity to return the original investment multiple times; the best that you can hope for with this specific strategy is 100% of the premium paid. In our case, this would mean keeping the entire $500 paid to you by an investor.

Now, remember three different events are likely to take place. Basically, the stock price could rise, descend, or stay the same. Now should the stock stay at the strike price or rise above it, you get to keep the full premium amount. Remember that this is your aim with this strategy.

However, should the stock fall below the strike price at expiration of the contract, then the stock will have to be purchased at a loss. The maximum loss that will be incurred should the stock price fall to $0 is $5,000.

Why Apply this Strategy?

There are a couple of reasons why traders pursue this strategy. The short put strategy is largely used by investors who strongly believe, based on insights, past data or analysis, that the stock price will go down. It is quite similar to someone seeking insurance because a seller will try to sell the premium so that they do not eventually have to pay any money should things not work out.

This strategy of selling short puts should be sparingly used because it almost always ends up with investors buying shares, yet this was not a part of the initial plan. Any stock whose price begins to fall can very easily deplete any premiums that are received from the sale of put options.

Investors sometimes adopt this strategy with the hope that the underlying stock's value will rise especially because the trade does not require any immediate financial input. However, this strategy is capped, which means your profits are limited, and any downfall experienced is quite substantial. Therefore, always proceed with caution whenever you consider using the short put strategy.

You can also use this strategy to receive a preferred buy price when the stocks are too costly. You can do this by selling put options based on an underlying stock with a low strike price. The low price is likely to attract buyers who would love to invest in the stock. For instance, let us take company ABC whose stock price is $50. You can sell put options at a price of $2 per share for a strike price of $40.

In this case, if the stock price falls below the strike price upon expiration, you will receive the stock. The investor, on the other hand, will pay $40 per share, which is the strike price, less $2 per share which is the premium already paid.

However, should the stock price stay above the indicated strike price upon expiration, then you get to keep the premium payment and repeat the same strategy all over again.

4. The Covered Call Options Trading Strategy

This is yet another basic trading strategy that is sometimes used by both traders and investors. The difference here is that this specific strategy consists of two distinct parts. As an investor, you will need to first own the underlying shares then create a call option based on the underlying stock and sell it.

You will basically award the buyer all the benefit of price appreciation above the indicated strike price. When applying this strategy, you will assume that the stock price is likely to go down slightly remain flat until expiration. This will, in essence, allow you to keep the premium paid by the buyer and also keep the shares.

As the investor, you will not only keep the stock, but you are free to repeat the process and write another call option if you so wish. There is a critical point that you need to note, though. For every 100 shares that you own, you will only be selling one single call. If you do not do this, then you will probably fall victim to short or naked calls and exposure to huge, uncapped losses in the event of the stock price rising.

Covered calls can transform an otherwise unpleasant option strategy, such as one with naked calls, into one that is safe for you and potentially rewarding. This is why sometimes this strategy is among the favorite for investors seeking to earn a regular income.

Any Potential Benefits or Cons?
Your profitability in this instance is limited to the premium paid by the buyer. In our case, the maximum premium amount is $500, so this is the maximum amount that you stand to gain should everything work out in your benefit. This will need the stock to remain at strike price or below.

However, should the stock price go up exceeding the strike price, then the option becomes a lot more expensive because it offsets most of the gains made by the stock. It also caps the upside which can mean low chances of profitability. Since the upside of this strategy is capped, you stand a high chance of suffering losses.

The problem here is that these are losses you would not have incurred had you not set up this option call. However, you do not get to lose any newly invested capital. The other challenge with this strategy is that you risk a complete loss of the stock's worth minus the $500 premium paid to you.

When Is This Strategy Adopted?
You can use the covered call option if you are an investor seeking to generate income but with limited risk even as you hope the share price will remain flat or fall just a bit until expiration.

You can also use the covered call strategy in order to get a higher sale price for your stocks. You can do this by lowering the premium cost as well as setting lucrative higher strike price. These will entice potential buyers to actually decide to purchase the call option. For instance, if the price of the stock of company ABC is $50, you can price these at a strike price of $60 then place a premium on each share of $2.

5. The Married Put Option Strategy
The married put options trading strategy is considered sophisticated, just like the covered call option strategy. Both are

thought to be more sophisticated compared to other basic options trading strategies.

This specific strategy is considered more complex because it combines two approaches. These are ownership of the underlying stock and a long put. It is these two that are "married together" and hence the name of the strategy. It is important to note the implications of adopting this or any other strategy.

With the married put, you get to purchase one put for every 100 shares of stock. This particular strategy allows you, as an investor, to own shares and hope to benefit from a rise in price.

It then goes further and offers you an opportunity to hedge your position should the stock price start to fall. This approach is quite similar to purchasing insurance as it charges you a premium to protect your investment from loss due to a decline in share price.

Potential Benefits and Downsides of This Strategy

The married put has some upsides to it. However, these depend on what happens to the stock price. Should this specific strategy allow you to continue with stock ownership as the price increases, then your profit level is potentially unlimited. All you will do is deduct the cost of the premium from your profits.

The option itself will benefit you if the price of the stock falls. This will essentially match any price decline and will offset stock loss less the premium which is capped at $500. As an investor, you are able to hedge against losses and keep holding the shares in the hope that the value will appreciate once the expiration date is attained.

The benefit of this specific put option strategy is that you can use it to hedge. As an investor, you will use this specific strategy if you are hoping that your stock price continues to appreciate. You also use the marriage put option when hoping to protect price gains that your stock makes as you hope and wait for further gains.

Chapter 10 - Learning How to Read an Options Chart

A lot of traders, and investors, have come to learn of the numerous benefits associated with options trading. Many more desire to become wealthy through options trading. This is why the trading volumes at options exchanges have increased steadily over the years.

Data dissemination and electronic trading have enabled more traders and investors to participate in options trading. To create wealth and generate a recurrent income from trading, it is important that you understand the trading process, terminology, and other useful features.

There are investors and traders who make use of options in order to speculation about price direction. Others use them in order to hedge either an anticipated or existing position while others come up with unique positions that offer irregular benefits. Such benefits are generally unavailable to regular traders.

For instance, as an options trader, you can earn profits should an underlying stock remain unchanged. One of the crucial elements of success when it comes to options trading is learning to select the correct option or even a combination. These are options that are essential for the creation of a position that harbors the appropriate risk-to-reward opportunities. To be successful and create substantial wealth you need to be a savvy trader. What you need to do at the options market is to find sophisticated data sets that will possibly earn you attractive rewards.

Previous Era Options Trading

Back in the past decade or so, options price reports were sent to newspapers. The newspapers would list a lot of rows of data. Most of the data was illegible and most people could not decipher its meaning. Such data was often printed in the financial sector of the newspapers. Today, however, traders are choosing to search for options data via online sources. Even as each source formats its data differently, the data and variables used are the ones found to be necessary and essential by today's traders.

Long Puts and Long Calls

There are several options positions that are commonly used. The simplest of them all is either a long put or a long call on its own.

• You stand to benefit greatly from this position if underlying asset's price as well as the downside remains limited to the premium.

• A straddle is created when you simultaneously purchase put options that have a similar strike price as well as expiration date. You will enjoy huge rewards if there is a rise or fall of the underlying asset's price. The only problem is that you get to lose money should the price remain relatively stable.

• We also have a strategy known as strangle. This is a strategy that is employed to purchase a call option and then a put option that has a lower strike. It is this put with a lower strike that gives this strategy its name, strangle. For this strategy to be successful then a large price movement either way is necessary.

• When you are short with either strangle or straddle strategies, you will make good money in a market with minimal movement. Being short simply means that you

Options Spreads Butterflies and Bulls

There are yet other trading strategies that are crucial for successful traders. These also have great potential and will guide you in making large amounts of money. These will essentially show you how to work with certain spreads. We can have a call or put spread created.

Put Spread: This spread is also known as a bear vertical spread. When dealing with this option type, you will buy a put option then sell another put option that has a lower strike price.

Call Spread: This kind of spread is also known as the bull vertical spread. You can create this spread option if you purchase a call option and at the same time sell a call option that has a larger strike price. You can profit from this kind of trade when there is an increase in the price of the underlying asset.

Calendar spread: Anytime that you buy and then sell options that have varying expiration times or dates, then these options are referred to as calendar spreads. It can also be called a time spread.

Butterflies

We can say that we have a butterfly spread where there exist options at three distinct strikes. These three strikes are equidistant to each other and the options at these points are all of a similar kind. This means they are either all puts or calls and have a similar expiration time.

We can have either a short or long butterfly. Where we have a long butterfly case, you should sell the middle strike option and then purchase the outside strikes. These are often bought at the ratio of 1:2:1. This simply means buy one, sell two and then buy another one. This ratio should hold at all times otherwise the situation will not be a butterfly.

One important factor that you need to keep in mind is that the butterfly's value will never get to zero.

Butterfly Spread Example

Let us look at an example involving the butterfly spread option. We will go long on a 70 call, then two short at 75 and then go long again with an 80 call option. For out identical trade, we could opt for the two short 75 puts, the long 70 put ad 80 put options. Since the butterfly formation is long, it will likely benefit from a market with little activity.

Using the spread example, we are able to create a synthetic position directly from the options. This kind of strategy is also referred to as the put-call parity. Simply put,

The Call Price – Put Price = Underlying Price – Strike Price

We can use the formula indicated above to come up with a synthetic long call. This is by simply rearranging it. Synthetic puts are simply a combination of a long call and shorting the underlying security. There are numerous ways of combining all sorts of spreads together with trade in the underlying tocks. By doing this, you will be able to achieve many novel positions like the risk reversal, fence, or even collar. These offer you numerous ways of making money.

Chapter 11 - Options Trading Q & A

What benefits come along with options trading?

Options are a type of stock derivative that offers better than average leverage for several reasons, starting with the fact that the overall cost to get started is far lower than with other investment options with similar leverage. Despite this fact, they make it possible to see serious returns in a relatively short period of time for those who make the right decisions in the right timeframe. The end result is that the risk that is present with options trading can be largely mitigated and at the very most you will never lose more than your initial investment. Traders often use put and call options as the vehicle of choice for ETFs, stocks and commodities.

How is trading options different than trading stocks?

The primary difference between trading stocks and trading options is the amount of time involved as all options have a built in expiration date which stocks do not have. To counter this downside, the leverage possible from options is far greater than that of stocks. For example, trading shares of Apple stock is likely outside the means of many but almost anyone has the ability to profit from options based around the same stock for far less buy-in.

Can I trade options for a living?

While the short answer is yes, the long answer is a bit more complex. Much like any other career, trading successfully requires lots of experience, patience, and practice. While some people will pick it up and see serious success straight away, those are in the extreme minority as the majority will experience few, if any, positive returns for at least the first month or so while they get the hang of the process. Furthermore, it is important to keep in mind that even the most successful traders don't have a successful trade percentage even close to 100 percent. If you make it to 60 percent then you might have what it takes to be a professional, but only if you have the capital to see you through the bad times when your luck has run out. Before you try and make a living trading options it is recommended that you have a significant amount of trading capital saved and that you have at least a year's worth of successful trading experience under your belt first.

How are options taxed?
The tax code is extremely complicated when it comes to investments in the stock market and adding options to the mix will only make things even more complicated still. While you may want to learn the ins and outs eventually, odds are you already have enough on your plate learning the basics of options trading which means that finding a tax professional who is already proficient in the nitty gritty will make your life much easier in both the short and the long-term.

Is it possible to trade options within an IRA?
Trading options as part of your IRA is really no different than trading them within a regular account with the exception that you are not allowed to take advantage of margin in any shape or form. As a result, all transactions are automatically

conducted through a cash account. It is important to keep in mind that naked selling from within an IRA account is illegal.

Is a traditional broker necessary in the age of the online trading platform?

While the online trading platform certainly makes parts of the process far more manageable, it is important to keep in mind that a physical broker is often responsible for more than just placing the trade which means they can add significant value to the process if used correctly. This is especially true with the Chicago Board as it has a larger concentration of market makers directly on the floor. Thus, floor brokers are able to use their personal connections and expertise to tap into liquidity that may not be accessible through more traditional channels. Likewise, when the order is placed the broker can be right there to represent it on the floor while the client is online as well. Thus, they are provided with a broader spectrum of coverage than might otherwise be the case while also scoping out two separate lines of liquidity at the same time.

Chapter 12 - Options on Other Instruments

While equity options are by far the most common, there are other options and instruments that are also widely used. Futures are more like European options than American because they require delivery of the underlying at the expiration date. There is no option to exercise or not (unless you consider selling the future back to the market as the option). Options can also be purchased on futures, and futures on options, because the financial world is full of innovation. Some of these may be custom only, though, so it may not be something heavily traded or easily found. Further, strategies can involve both futures and options on equities or anything else, since complexity can be used to reduce risk or increase profit.

Futures are used between companies and suppliers, but you can also profit from them. Forex is also used between companies and within companies, but if you have high leverage, forex is also an avenue for you. Options on forex exist, and you can use the same strategies here for forex and futures as you would on equity.

Fixed income, otherwise known as bonds, is also a market for options. Fixed income is much steadier than its potentially volatile futures, forex, and equity markets, so you may not be able to generate as much profit here as in the other markets, but it is still a market to look at if you have experience in FI or have an interest in it.

Keep in mind that equity is highly liquid and does not take a lot of capital to get started in, and as such, equity is probably the best place for a new options trader to start. Whether it be binary, index, single stock, ETF, private stock, or any other equity style, you can use the above strategies to profit or insure. That does not discount the fact, though, that one may use the above strategies and the myriad others found online to trade the other types of financial instruments. Large institutions have customized options on arcane instruments like collateralized debt obligations and credit default swaps. As an individual, it is highly unlikely you will be dealing with these. However, if you are a student or otherwise interested in the financial world, you may want to read up more on this or even pursue this as your future career path.

Chapter 13 - Differences Among Forex, Stocks and Options

There are different reasons some traders love to use forex instead of the stock market. One of them is the forex leverage.

We will look at the disparities that exist between forex trading and stock trading.

1.   Leverage

When it comes to stock trading, you tend to trade with a cap of leverage of two to one. You must have some requirements on the ground before these can be done. It is not every investor than ends up being approved for that margin account, and this is what a trader needs to be leveraged in a typical stock market.

When it comes to forex trading, the entire system is totally different. Before you can trade using leverage, you need to have opened the forex trading account. That's the only requirement that is out there, nothing else. When you open a forex account, you can easily use the leverage feature.

If you are trading in the United States of America, you will be restricted to a leveraging of 50:1 leveraging. Countries outside of the US are restricted to leverage of about 200:1. It is better when you are outside the US, than in the US.

2.   Liquidity differences

When you decide to trade stocks, you end up purchasing the companies' shares that have a cost from a bit of dollars down to even hundreds of dollars. Usually, the price in the market tends to share with demand and supply.

3. Paired trades

When you trade with forex, you are facing another world, unseen in the stock market. Though the currency of a country tends to change, there will always be a great supply of currency that you can trade. What this means is that the main currencies in the world tend to be very liquid.

When you are in forex trading, you will see that the currencies are normally quoted in pairs. They are not quoted alone. This means that you should be interested in the country's economic health that you have decided to trade in. The economic health of the country tends to affect the worth of the currency.

The basic considerations change from one forex market to the next. If you decide to purchase the Intel shares, the main aim is to see if the stock's value will improve. You aren't interested in how the prices of other stocks are.

On the other hand, if you have decided to sell or buy forex, you need to analyze the economies of those countries that are involved in the pairs.

You should find out if the country has better jobs, GDP, as well as political prospects.

To do a successful trade in the Forex market, you will be expected to analyze not only one financial entity, but two.

The forex market tends to show higher level of sensitivity in upcoming economic and political scenarios in many countries.

You should note that the U.S. stock market, unlike many other stock markets is not so sensitive to a lot of foreign matters.

4. Price sensitivity to trade activities

When we look at both markets, we have no choice but to notice that there is varying price sensitivity when it comes to trade activities done.

If a small company that has fewer shares has about ten thousand shares bought from it, it could go a long way to impact the price of the stock. For a big company such as Apple, such n number of shares when bought from it won't affect the stock price.

When you look at forex trades, you will realize that trades of a few hundreds of millions of dollars won't affect the major currency at all. If it affects, it would be minute.

5.   Market accessibility

It is easy to access the currency market, unlike its counterpart, the stock market. Though you may be able to trade stocks every second of the day, five days weekly in the twenty first century, it is not easy.

A lot of retail investors end up trading via a United States brokerage that makes use of a single major trading period every day, which spans from 9:30 AM to 4:00 PM. They go ahead to have a minute trading hour past that time, and this period has price and volatility issues, which end up dissuading a lot of retail traders from making use of such time.

Forex trading is different. One can carry out such trading every second of the day because there are a lot of forex exchanges in the world, and they are constantly trading in one time zone or the other.

Forex Trading Vs Options

A trader may believe the United States Dollar will become better when compared to the Euro, and if the results pan out, the person earns.

The strategy, if it works, can help in affecting the trade when the research pans out.

When you get involved in Options Trading, you tend to get involved in the purchase and sales of options on great amounts of futures, stocks and so on, that will move either up or below at a price during the phase.

It is similar to Forex Trading, since you can easily leverage the buying power to have a controlling power on futures or stocks.

There exist a number of disparities that exist between Options trading and Forex trading. They are:

1.   24 Hour Trading:

When you get involved in Forex instead of Options trading, you have the capability of trading every second of the day, five days weekly. When you look at the Forex market, you will realize that it lives longer than any financial market in the world.

If you have decided to get double digit gains in the market, it is important to possess a generous amount of time every week to carry out these trades. If a large event occurs anywhere in the world, you may end up being amongst the first to benefit from the situation in the Foreign Exchange market.

You don't expect to spend time waiting and hoping that the market opens in the market like in the case of trading options.

With Forex, you can easily trade anytime you want, at all times of the night and day. Whenever you wish, you can trade it.

2.   Rapid Trade Execution:

When you immediately make use of the Forex market; you tend to get instantaneous trade executions. You don't have to be delayed like in the case of Options or some other markets too.

When you place the order, it ends up being filled using the best potential price in the market, instead of wondering what price ends up being ordered.

You won't have to have the urge to slip like the case of options. When you are involved in Foreign Exchange Trading, there is a great chance of liquidity unlike in the case of Options trading.

3.   No Commissions:

Forex market is one that doesn't need commission because it acts as an inter-bank market, where buyers are matched with sellers instantly.

There aren't cases of brokerage fees like in the stock market and other markets.

You will see a spread that exists between ask price and the bid, that is the way a lot of Forex trading firms earn their money.

What this means is that when you trade Forex, you stand to save the brokerage fees unlike in the case of options trading, where you are expected to pay communion since you have no choice but to use a brokerage firm.

Forex Trading Risks

Like every financial market out there, there are risks that one may have to face. The interbank market is known to have different degrees of regulations. Apart from that, forex instruments aren't as standardized as other financial market instruments out there. Do you know that in some parts of the globe, there are no regulations to the forex market?

The interbank market consists of different banks all over the world trading with one another.

The banks have no choice but to determine an asset to credit risk and sovereign risks. They have come up with different internal processes, in a bid to ensure that they remain quite safe. These types of regulations are imposed in the industry to ensure that every participating bank is protected.

The market pricing comes from the forces of demand and supply because the market is made up of different banks giving bids and offers.

The fact that there is a great amount of trade flows in the market means that rogue investors can't influence the worth of a currency. This ensures that there is transparency in the foreign exchange market for those traders that are privy to interbank dealing.

A lot of countries have regulations concerning the forex, but not all do.

Pros and Cons of Forex

First Pro:

When it comes to a daily trading volume in every market out there, the forex is the largest, meaning that it possesses the largest amount of liquidity.

This is one reason that one can easily enter or exit a position whenever he wants, for a small spread in a lot of market conditions.

Cons:

Brokers, banks and dealers are known to give a great level of leverage, meaning that investors can easily control huge positions using a tiny amount of money.

Though you don't see it every time, a high ratio of leverage of 100:1 is possible to see in the foreign exchange market. It is important that a trader knows how to use leverage, as well as the risks that using leverage brings to an account. Using a large amount of leverage has forced a lot of dealers to become bankrupt unexpectedly.

Second Pro

You can trade in the foreign exchange market every second of the day, six days in a week. It usually begins daily in Australia and ends in New York.

The main centers for forex are Singapore, Hong Kong, Sydney, Tokyo, New York, London and Paris.

Second Con

Before you can trade currencies in a profitable manner, you have to understand economic indicators and basics. A currency investor has to possess a great understanding of how a lot of economies function, as well as how connected they are. You need to understand these fundamentals that are able to alter the values of currencies.

What Is A Stock

Stock is sometimes called equity or shares. This is a kind of security that shows proportionate ownership when the firm that issues it is concerned. When a person has stocks, he/she is entitled to a proportion of the earnings and assets of the company.

One can buy stocks and sell them on stock exchanges, but this doesn't mean that there aren't other ways of buying and selling stocks. Stocks can also be exchanged in private sales. There is hardly any investor in the financial world that doesn't have stocks in their portfolio.

Before the transactions can be said to be legitimate, they must be in line with the government regulations that have been put in place to shield investors from fraudulent processes.

When compared to a lot of financial instruments, stocks have overshadowed them.

Stock Vs Bond

Companies give out stocks to raise the needed capital to improve their business or get involved in new projects.

Shares can be gotten in different ways. Sometimes, a person may purchase it directly from the firm when it issues it in the primary market. In other cases, the investor may purchase it in the secondary market from another shareholder. Whenever you see a corporation issuing shares, know that it carries it out because it wants to raise money.

Bonds are in another world of its own. Bondholders are seen as creditors to the firm, and they tend to get interest instead of dividends. They are also paid the principal.

When it comes to stakeholders in a company, creditors have more right over the assets and earnings than shareholders when bankruptcy occurs.

The corporation is expected to pay shareholders first before it pays shareholders during a bankruptcy. Shareholders end up being the last in line and may end up getting nothing or a little amount. What this means is that stocks have higher risks than bonds.

If you can't stomach this, you should avoid going for stocks.

What are The Options

Options are those contracts that allow the bearer to be involved in the purchase or sales of a stipulated amount of asset at a fixed price. The bearer has the choice to buy or not, as long as the contract hasn't expired.

Options are bought like a lot of asset classes by making use of brokerage investment accounts.

Options are strong to the extent that they can improve the portfolio of an individual. They can get this done by leverage and added income protection.

Based on the scenarios at hand, different option situations can suit the goals of an investor.

Let's say a stock market is declining; options can be used as an effective hedge to clamp down on downside losses. One can use options to get recurring income. They can also be utilized for speculative purposes like wagering on where the stock price would go.

The way that free lunch doesn't exist in bonds and stocks is the same way that there is no free lunch with options.

There are some risks that one may face when options trading is concerned. You have to understand these risks before you jump into options trading.

This is one reason that when you have decided to trade options with a brokerage company, you are shown a disclaimer that is similar to this:

Options are members of a bigger league of securities, which are called derivatives. The price of a derivative is linked to the price of another thing. Let's make things more transparent. The derivative of a tomato is ketchup. The derivative of grapes is wine. The derivative of a stock is a stock option.

Options can be said to be derivatives of financial securities, meaning that their worth is dependent on another asset's price.

Some examples of derivatives are puts, calls, forwards, futures, and so on.

Call and Put Options

When we say that options are derivative securities, we mean that their price is related to the pricing of another thing. This means that the other thing is what controls the price of the options.

If you purchase the options contract, you are given the right to buy or sell an asset at a stimulate price before the deal expires. You aren't under compulsion to do this.

When a person has a call option, he is given the right to purchase a stock. On the other hand, when a person is given a put option, he has the right to sell the stock.

You can see the call option as a form of down-payment for something that can be gotten in the future.

Let's use a more explicit example. A person sees a new building going up. He may want to have the right to buy it later but says he won't buy it until it has gotten to some stage, or some other condition has been met, this is an example of an option. He can decide to use the option or not. He isn't under compulsion.

Let's say the developer agrees to give the person the right to purchase the house for about a million dollars at any time within the next three years. Before the developer can agree with this, the prospective buyer has to pay a down payment, which can't be refundable. Within that period of three years, the developer isn't allowed to sell the house to anyone else, until after the term expires.

Chapter 13 - The Basic Butterfly Spread Strategy

As you saw from the beginner's guide to options trading (if you read by beginner's guide), it's largely advised to new investors to options trading that he or she should start the purchasing process through simple calls and puts that offer little in terms of reward. The fact of the matter is that over time, the beginner options trader is going to start looking elsewhere for higher returns and lower levels of risk, as long as he or she sticks with options trading for a while and gets the hang of how the market works. This chapter is going to discuss the basic version of the butterfly spread strategy. After you are aware of both of these types of strategies, you can then decide for yourself which type you'd like to use. If you're a timid options trading investor, you might choose to simply figure out the ins and outs of the basic butterfly spread, while if you're more a "need for speed" type person, the modified butterfly spread may be right up your ally.

How the Basic Butterfly Spread Works

Short call butterfly example

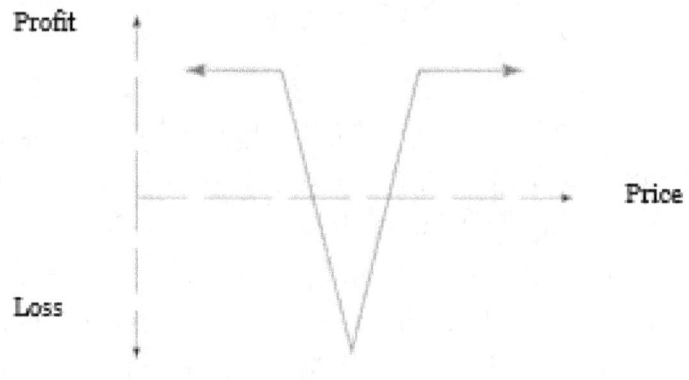

Profit

Loss

Price

Long call butterfly spread example

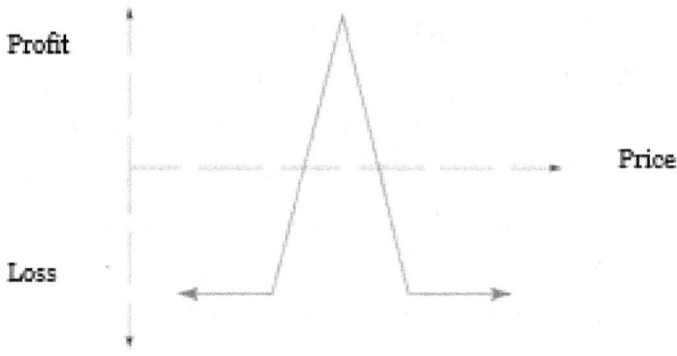

Profit

Loss

Price

Before we look at the more advanced version of the butterfly spread, we are first going to look at the basics of the strategy. The first concept that you have to understand about the butterfly spread strategy is that it's implemented using a specific ratio of calls to puts, with the ratio being 1:2:1. This strategy can be used with calls or with puts, but you are only using one type of option for your specific strategy. For example, if you decide that you want to focus on calls you would buy one call at a specific strike price, sell two other calls at an even higher strike price, and then buy one more call at the highest strike price of all. Contrastingly, if you decided instead to focus your attention on calls instead of puts, this would mean that you would buy one put at a certain strike price, then sell two at a lower strike price, and then buy one more put option at the lowest price of all. Moreover, it's important to remember that there are going to always be one call or put on either side of two other calls or puts, depending on which type of option you're interested in purchasing and selling. If you stop to think about the name of the concept, it might even seem as if the 1's for the ratio are the wings of the butterfly, while the 2's for the ratio is the butterfly's body. While this isn't a definite reason as to why the butterfly spread got its name, it might a useful tool or image to use when thinking about what the butterfly spread is all about. More succinctly, below is a comprehensive recap of the butterfly spread ratio:

1 Call (or 1 Put): 2 Calls (or 2 Puts): 1 Call (or 1 Put)

Hopefully seeing the ratio spelled out in front of you can help you to understand this concept to the best of your ability. Additionally, the arrow underneath of the ratio has been placed there as a reminder that the first call (or put) on the left should always have the smallest strike price, while the call (or put) all the way to the right should always have the largest strike price. This is an important concept to grasp when dealing with the butterfly spread, and if you overlook it then it's likely that you will end up losing money and your strategy will fail you. It's safe to no one is interested in that sort of outcome.

In order for the basic butterfly spread to be successful, the strike price of the options being sold (so the two options in the middle) should have strike prices that are close to the current price of the underlying security. The other two securities that you're purchasing should be at opposite ends of the spectrum, meaning that the one on the left will be below the current market price for the stock and the one on the right will be above the current market price. Positioning your options in this manner will allow you to create a potentially "neutral" position for yourself where you will be able to make money within the butterfly as long as the price of the underlying security stays within a range that is below as well as above the current market price. Remember, an underlying security is the option that you're either looking to purchase or sell, it's not the share of the company itself. The point of the basic butterfly spread is to create a sort of profit range so that there is not merely one certain price on which a share must fall in order for you to be profitable. By creating a range of numbers that will lead to success, you have a higher likelihood of walking away with a profit than you would if you were to only purchasing or sell one put or call and hope for the best.

The butterfly spread technique is largely considered to be neutral in quality. Being "neutral" in your stock market strategy does not mean that you don't have an opinion or that you are choosing to keep your opinion secret; rather, being neutral in your options trading strategy means that as an investor you are strategizing in a way that will cause you to benefit from both increasing as well as decreasing prices in the market. The primary reason that investors will give for behaving in this manner is that they are trying to avoid certain types of risks. It's generally assumed that when you decide to act as a neutral party in the stock market, that you are able to diminish some of the risk that is associated with a negotiation because whether or not the market swings in a certain direction, you are going to potentially profit from it. It's important to note here that there is no one distinct way to be market neutral. The best market-neutral practitioners are able to take any momentum in the market and have it work to his or her benefit.

Other Facts about the Butterfly Spread

Some other miscellaneous factors that it's important to understand about the butterfly spread is that all of the four options that are used for this strategy should have the same expiration date. Another critically important factor that you need to be thinking about as you pick out options with the proper strike prices for your butterfly is that these prices should be the same distance from the middle strike price at which you are selling stocks. For example, let's say that you decide to sell two options at a strike price that's set a sixty-dollars. If you made the decision to purchase this middle-of-the-road strike price, then you're going to have to purchase one option on either side at fifty-five dollars and sixty-five dollars, respectively. This way, the investor (you) will profit from the transaction as long as the underlying asset's price stays between fifty-five and sixty-five dollars. If the underlying asset price ends up being exactly on either of these numbers, then the investor is going to realize the maximum level of loss; however, any money amount between these two numbers would lead to some sort of profit for the investor.

Chapter 14 - How to Keep a Day Trading Journal and Why It's Important

As was already stated before we started our discussion on specific advanced day trading strategies, it might be necessary for you to go back and reevaluate the key points of each one before you actually start to use it in a real-time setting. Now that you have a basic understanding of two advanced strategies that many day traders use on a regular basis, we are going to turn attention away from the technicalities of strategies and towards the idea of recordkeeping. One of the things that many experienced day traders tout is the importance of keeping some sort of trade journal. This chapter will focus on what to include in a trade journal and why it's important. Let's take a look at what you should be including in your trade journal, and then we will focus on why it's important to create one and upkeep it.

What Should You Be Including in Your Trade Journal?

1. Did Your Trade Work as You Expected It To?

One of first aspects that you need to consider as you look to write entries into your trade journal is whether or not the trade worked out in the same way that you originally thought it would. Often times when trading on the stock market, things have a tendency to not go as planned. If you find that this is the case when you're making deals for yourself, then you need to address the areas that strayed from what you had in your head before the trading began. While you're documenting this information, it's important to keep in mind that often times the strategy behind your trade can differ from what actually happens when there's money as stake. Again, this could be for a variety of reasons, including the fact that emotions could be influencing the trades that you're making. Be open to being honest with yourself about whether or not a trade went right or wrong. This will help you to see not only your areas of weakness but also your areas of strength and this will help you in your overall long-term stock strategies

2. What is Your Stop Limit and Why Did You Set It There?

Once you've documented whether or not your trade strategy work out as you intended it to, the next concept that you should be documenting is your stop limit. Your stop limit is the amount of money that you're willing to lose in a trade. Often times, even seasoned investors in the heat of the moment will stray from their stop limit because they are eager to make money where it doesn't exist. Documenting what your stop limit is, the reason why you set it there, and whether or not you stuck to your stop limit can help you to figure out how disciplined you are in sticking to your stock market strategy over the course of the day and whether or not you need to check yourself as the day progresses. Another reason why documenting this type of information is important is because it will most likely ultimately lead you to realizing that you need to have a firm grasp on how much money you're going to be spending throughout the day on each investment. Again, this aspect of the trading journey is mostly there to reinforce the idea of discipline into your trading strategy.

3. What Did You Choose to Trade and Why?

Lastly, one of the key elements that is included into any successful and serious investor's trade journal is documentation of which stocks they traded throughout the day and why. So many investors back up their investment strategies with reasons that include that the price of a particular stock has risen or fallen to the amount that is "just right", without backing it up with any substantial information. This isn't a good type of strategy, and writing down your reasoning for purchasing a particular stock will help you to see whether or not your stock choices are grounded in substantial logic. What's even worse is that sometimes traders will choose to purchase and sell stock out of merely a feeling of boredom. This too can end up having disastrous consequences. It's likely that a trader may not be aware of the fact that he or she is trading out of boredom or because the market is moving "just right" for them, and often times having a trade journal will force these people to be awakened to these types of facts. This is yet another reason why a trade journal can be beneficial.

Why is a Trade Journal Important?

Now that you know that you should be including in your trade journal, this next section of the chapter is going to look at why trade journals are important. Hopefully after reading this section, you will be able to see why you need to start using one. One of the great things about the prevalence of computers is that you can easily create templates for yourself and quickly insert this information at the end of each trading day. Even if you are not that thrilled about documenting your experience as a day trader at the end of each trading day, you should still be willing to do it at least once a week. Now that you have hopefully come to understand the type of information the is generally found in a trade journal, let's take a look at some of the reasons why a trade journal can be beneficial to you.

Reason 1 Why You Need a Trade Journal: Review

Some of the best day traders go over their trade journal in the morning before they start their trades for the rest of the day. By doing this, they are clearing and focusing their mind on the mistakes and good things that they did the day before. Another good tactic that the top traders typically implement is that they will write down key notes that they learned at the end of the day for that particular day. Over time, you will be able to simply look at the key information from each day, and this will eliminate the need to sift through entire pages of information when you've for what you're looking. Over time and day-by-day, you will be growing and educating yourself as an investor, and this activity only takes a few moments each morning.

Reason 2 Why You Need a Trade Journal: Improvement

The second reason why you really should be considering keeping a trading journal if you're not already is because it gives you the ability to improve upon areas of yourself and your trading patterns. For example, successful investors will usually take the time to look at the points when they entered and exited a trade in order to figure out whether or not they could have improved these points with the information they had at that particular moment in time. This is the type of contemplation that often separates the winners from the losers, and a day trading journal is where it at all starts.

Reason 3 Why You Need a Trade Journal: Emotional Check

The last reason why you should consider keeping a day trading journal is so that you can keep your emotions in check. Emotional trading is often one of the aspects of trading that many investors forget about, but it can also be the silent killer that causes deals to go south. It might even be beneficial for you to document each day the emotions that were surrounding particular decisions, so that you can focus some of your energy on eliminating these feelings over time.

Chapter 15 - Price Action Patterns

As a beginner, I do not recommend getting into pure price action since this is a skill that is fairly advanced and rushing into it is a surefire way to confuse yourself. There are some beginner friendly price action methods however which I recommend for their simplicity and ease of application. My personal opinion is that price action is ultimately the only way to successfully trade the markets since by reading price, we're only a step removed from the order flow. Nothing else offers us a closer look in the FX markets since the order book is unavailable.

The 3 main price action patterns you need to be aware of, as a beginner, are:

1) Inside Bars (IB)

2) Pin Bars (PB)

3) 2 Bar Reversal (2B/Revs)

Before we begin, let me re-iterate something which I've already done multiple times. The strategies listed here are of use only if you understand and trade in line with the principles of trend strength. You cannot blindly take, for example, every single IB that presents itself. You need to understand the specific environments in which such patterns work and most of all you must understand this: The patterns are powerful because the underlying price mechanics and order flow create them. They aren't powerful because of their shape or because of how pretty they look. In my experience, most traders understand this intellectually but fail to implement this when trading. You need to start off by determining the trend strength and the price environment (turning points etc) and then start looking for entry signals. The environment determines which signals you look for.

Now that that's clear, lets move on. We will first tackle the inside bar.

Inside Bars

The inside bar is a fairly straight forward pattern to spot. The entire pattern consists of 2 bars, with the bar to the left engulfing the bar to the right. The bar on the right is referred to as an inside bar since it seems to be "inside" the bar to the left. This pattern is best used as a trend continuation indicator, that is, in environments where the trend strength is increasing and the counter trend players are steadily being overwhelmed. An understanding of the price mechanics behind this pattern will give a clearer picture of why this is so.

As trend strength continues to increase and as the market becomes ever more imbalanced to one side, the counter trend players' strength continually diminishes. Eventually it reaches a point where the players on one side of the market are so forceful that all the counter trend players can muster is a cursory effort at repelling the opposite side. This presents itself as a small bar which goes against the trend and is unable to match the bar that preceded it. The with trend order flow is so strong that sometimes the counter trend players fail to even register a single bar in their favor and only manage to slightly halt proceedings.

Inside Bar Patterns

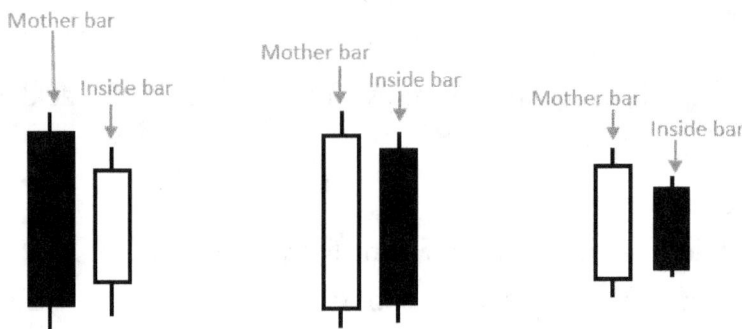

Such a temporary halt gives us a great indication of where to hop on board the trend and ride it to profits. When looking at this pattern you want the bar on the left to be in the direction of the trend, that is, if we're in a bull trend, the bar on the left should be a bullish one. If a bear trend, then the bar on the left should be a bearish one. The direction of the inside bar, or bar on the right, doesn't matter as long as it satisfies the requirement that its entirety, including any wicks and tails, is confined within the boundaries of the bar on the left.

Remember to use this pattern only in strongly trending environments or in instances where the trend strength is clearly becoming more and more biased towards one side. Another rookie mistake to avoid is to blindly see that a bar has printed inside the one to its left and neglect the trend direction of the previous bar. It needs to be with trend always. There will be times when a bar will be inside the bar on the left but its body will be almost the same size. In these cases, its best to ignore the pattern since it indicates the underlying price mechanics are not favorable. If you can understand the underlying mechanics, you will understand what optimizes this pattern.

The best way to enter, according to me, is to place a stop order just beyond the bar on the left so you're targeting an entry on the break of the high or low of that bar, in the direction of the trend. An aggressive stop placement would be just past the high or low of the inside bar, depending on the direction of the trade. A more conservative placement would be above the high or low of the bar on the left. Play around with both methods on paper and see which strategy fits you best. When I say fits you, I don't mean which one you're comfortable with, I'm referring to which stop placement makes you more money. Target at least 1.5-2X risk with this pattern. Usually, you'll find price runs a lot further so look at taking a partial exit at a 2X reward and trailing your stop downward thereafter. I don't recommend beginners take partial exits though.

You may read in some places that IBs are a great indicators of reversals as well. While this may have been observed by certain "authorities", in my experience, this is never the case and simply leads to more confusion. Stick to using inside bars as a continuation signal and you'll make more money than most. There's no need to complicate things unnecessarily.

Pin Bars

The term pin bar refers to a candle which has either a tail at the bottom or a wick at the top. Generally accepted convention is that the body of the pin should be less than a third of the entire length of the bar. I'm not a fan of mathematical boundaries like these since it doesn't make sense to restrict yourself but suffice to say, just look at the bar. If it feels like its a pin visually, go ahead and take it without getting hung up on bar proportion calculations.

It is important to understand what the underlying price mechanics are when it comes to a pin bar. Let's say we're in a price move and as it exhausts itself, the counter trend players start pushing back with increasing strength. The pin bar with a wick represents a case where sellers have started pushing against the bulls and the bar with a tail represents the opposite, that is, the bulls pushing back against the bears. Just like with the inside bar, it is important to realize that the pin bar is a result of underlying price mechanics and isn't a cause of order flow in any direction. So it always pays to analyze the price environment from a trend strength perspective.

Pin Bar Patterns

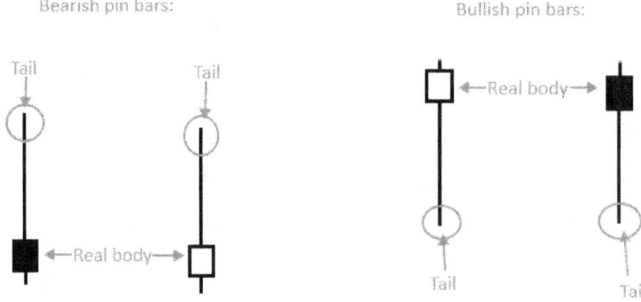

Given the preceding description, it should become clear that the pin bar is a reversal indicator. Now here comes the tricky bit. The best way to use this pattern is as a trend continuation one. This will be confusing and those of you who have used and studied pin bars previously from existing "authorities" out there will not have thought of using them in this way. The best way to trade is to trade with the trend, especially if you're a beginner. It doesn't make sense to take the hard route when an easier one is available. So how does one use a reversal pattern to predict a continuation?

Before I elaborate I want to point out something. And here I am, saying use this particular reversal pattern as a continuation one. The reason is this: The cup and handle involves a significant number of price bars and encompasses a lot of order flow within its confines. This gives us a substantial body of work within which we can judge the prevalent conditions and increases our odds of predicting a reversal. A pin bar, in contrast, is merely 1 bar. What makes you think 1 bar is more special than the next one in any market? Even the significance of important event bars diminishes within an hour of their occurrence. So how on earth can one pin bar decide and cement the case for a reversal of a trend which as been running for say 20-30 bars?

This applies to all timeframes and again illustrates how blind application of indicators without understanding order flow results in losses and in traders blaming the pattern when in reality, it is the trader that doesn't understand the nature of the market. Don't be that person who blindly applies indicators expecting some sort of magic solution that unlocks market secrets. The markets are far too chaotic and nuanced for one bar to ever have magical properties.

Having got that out of the way, lets proceed. The key to using this pattern is to understand that all trends have some form of imbalance in them. The degree varies but there are always counter trend players present looking to press their case. No market can exist without the other side. In a high trend strength environment, the counter players hardly get a look in and need to get out of the way quickly. As the steam begins to run out of the with trend players though, the counter players force periods where price goes sideways or maybe even retraces a bit before the with trend players wake up and the push continues. In these sideways movements or pauses, the orders are fairly evenly distributed, even though it may be for a short time and indeed, in some of them, the counter trend players may even have the upper hand for the time being. It is a reversal of this, counter trend, order flow that will indicate when the larger trend is ready to resume and the with trend players are ready to continue onward. It is important for you to understand this so take your time to absorb what has been said here.

A pin bar in such sideways environments or areas where the trend pauses, indicates a reversal of the sideways/counter trend flow and thus a continuation of the larger trend. This is the correct way of using a pin bar pattern. Common wisdom is to specify that pin bars signify reversals and everybody rushes to declare pin bars as the ultimate predictors of a trend which has lost steam. It is a mistake which I have made myself in the past. Your odds of success are extremely low to non existent if you think a single bar can reverse order flow biased towards a particular direction. If you find yourself thinking this way, your understanding of trend strength is inadequate and I recommend more practice with this. Always remember, that these patterns are simply to help with our entry timing. They do not dictate or cause any order flow by themselves.

An entry on the close of the pin bar with a stop below or above the wick/tail or closest support/resistance is the best entry method. Aim for at least a 2X reward with this and more advanced traders can take partial exits and trail their stops. The charts on the following pages will illuminate pin bars further.

2 Bar Reversals

2 bar reversals are another powerful reversal pattern which we will use as a continuation one much like the pin bar. The pattern itself is fairly easy to spot and consists of 2 bars which are mirror image of each other. If the bar on the left is a bullish one which closes right near its highs, the bar on the right is a bearish one which closes near its lows. Ideally, we want 2 bars with strong closes, that is, near their highs and lows and no wicks or tails. The term mirror image might confuse some beginners so let's break this down some more.

A 2 bar reversal is, from an order flow perspective, the exact same as a pin bar, except the reversal occurs over 2 bars instead of one. Indeed, if you imagine both the bars as one combined, the result will look like a pin bar. This is the best of way of determining whether or not a couple of bars form this pattern. This might seem tedious at first but with practice, you will be able to automatically spot it. The important thing to understand here is what the pattern tells us about the order flow, instead of looking at it as some sort of magical shape.

Since this is essentially a pin bar, playing out over two bars instead of one, the rules of the pin bar bar apply here as well and this is traded the same way. Aim for atleast a 2X reward with this pattern. The charts on the following pages illustrate this.

Final Words on PBs and 2B/Revs

While the charts I've displayed here to illustrate how these bars are traded are quite clean and clear, in reality, you will find a large number of pins and 2b/revs being thrown up in the markets. It will be confusing as to which signals you ought to take and which ones to discard. Well, your wait is over.

The key to picking the best pins and 2b/revs is to look for them in appropriate trend strength environments, when price is moving sideways in a trend. This means we need to look for them in environments with either strong or medium trend strength. Those environments where the counter trend players are clearly becoming stronger, you need to stay away from since the order flow is far too balanced for a couple of bars or one bar to have any significant impact. In other words, we want to look for these signals in environments where price only needs a small provocation to resume the trend it was in. This means, you do not use these signals to predict breakouts. It should also be evident now why we do not use these as reversal signals since at the point of reversal, order flow is largely balanced.

The demarcation line between a trend which has a strength of medium versus say weak-medium is up to you to determine based on your experience and comfort level. I've highlighted this because I personally feel comfortable taking this signal. If you're starting out, this is an advanced entry to take and an intimidating one and I recommend you stay away from such entries until you build up your skills via practice.

Master trend strength and get comfortable with it and you'll see your quality of trades skyrocket.

Chapter 16 - Tailoring Binary Options

When binary options come to mind, most people think of numbers. It's completely logical to do so, but an investor knows that trading is not as clean cut as that. This is one motive why people succeed at binary options trading, and others do not, and the reason goes further than the elements of a prosperous trader that have been already been stated. To become successful at trading binary options, it is not enough to just follow the rules; investors must be able to personalize them.

Tailoring Options

This book has already gone over the types of binary options available for trading, which include stocks, indices, commodities, and currency/forex. However, since the goal here is to come up with viable options for beginners, it would be best to discard the last two options. That leaves investment newcomers with stocks and indices, which, depending upon the perspective, are more or less the same thing. This is because indices can be made up of lists of the most popular stocks on the market versus a stock exchange may contain any number and variety of stocks regardless of their volatility, popularity, or accessibility. The terminology of trading on stock exchanges versus indices will come into play when selecting what is best for the individual.

So what is best? That will depend upon the existing trading abilities of the beginner and his or her interests. If the individual does have some background in trading, such as taking an active part in the growth of a mutual fund, then he or she may want to look into trading on a stock exchange using different stocks that may be a bit less well known and will help to diversity his or her profile. However, if the individual has no experience in investment, which is more likely to be the case, then it may be better to either trade on indices with extremely well-known stocks or to select well-known stocks from a stock exchange. In addition to this, there is a third option: depending upon the brokerage or platform the individual is trading on, it is possible to get a package deal that will allow the individual to trade on both the stock exchange and indices at the same time.

When selecting a platform, take into consideration which stocks to use. Again, investors should start out only trading on stocks with which they are familiar. Readers should determine their familiarity with companies by examining their lives: what products is the reader familiar with, whether that is technology, transportation, sports, energy, or healthcare? Additionally, take time zones into account. If a trader is living in Seattle but is trading on The New York Stock Exchange, then he or she will either need to be at the computer and ready to call the broker at 6:30am Pacific time or set up an automatic trader to begin the process when the bell rings on the exchange floor in New York. Although this latter option can be helpful, it is always best for a trader to look at the data personally.

Another factor that may play into selecting options is to examine time frame charts. This can be somewhat difficult because oftentimes companies will only allow someone to study the charts after the individual has become a customer. The positive note is that most reputable brokerages have access to a wide variety of stocks to choose from and so new investors should hopefully be able to select suitable stocks without examining the charts. However, once a trader has access to them, he or she should study them in order to determine which stocks have the highest rate of volatility. Stocks that make larger moves may prove easier to predict or at least have a higher chance of producing a result within a short span of time. However, traders should be warned that while this can be a practical method, it is also an ambitious one since trends can reverse themselves, especially in volatile climates. Consequently, establishing an exit point beforehand is recommended.

Above all, options should be limited to companies that interest the individual. If an investor is getting into binary options trading in order to make money and not because they love it then trading can be extremely difficult. Things will be easier if the investor chooses companies that are appealing. If a new investor loves the finance world then well-suited stocks will only make the process of reaping rewards more enjoyable.

Opportunities to Win

This is just one of the more difficult aspects of being a binary options trader. Usually, binary options only involve a yes or no choice: yes the trend will rise above the strike price or no, it won't. Spotting binary options trading opportunities, however, takes constant active participation on the trader's part. In order to take advantage of the opportunities the market provides; one must keep their ear to the financial ground.

An ideal way to do this is with newspapers. Investors should read financial sections of newspapers every day whether online or in print. Over time investors develop a preference for particular periodicals, but a wide range will help to broaden new investors' knowledge and make them more able to spot potential market indicators. Some may question the practicality behind reading the entirety of the financial news when only a portion of it may be directly related to the investor's interests, but the truth is that the financial world is deeply interconnected. If a trader is dealing in healthcare stocks, a huge fluctuation in another area such as homeownership could have a drastic effect on the stocks. It is always better to be aware of the whole financial picture and then hone in on a specific point than only be knowledgeable of one area. Additionally, it is just as important to see how a market closes for the day, as it is to see how it opens. An effective investor should be aware of financial news all day, not just in the morning.

An additional way to stay in touch with the financial world is through websites and blogs. Some great ones include Google Finance and CNN Money. A great financial resource can also be found in Investopedia, which is exactly what the name sounds like: a comprehensive and understandable encyclopedia for investment. Some of these websites have apps that will allow investors to receive alerts on their phones when a significant financial event occurs. Of course, investors will get a taste for their own preferred websites as they become more comfortable in the finance world.

Opportunities at Home

Perhaps the most alluring aspect of binary options trading is what it allows investors to do with their lives. Starting out in investment can be difficult; during lunch breaks and after work an investor may be constantly checking in on his or her investments or even may be changing his or her work schedule in order to accommodate trading. If the trader works hard enough and shows a talent for trading, eventually this will pay off and hopefully the trader will be able to quit his or her day job in order to primarily trade. Ideally the investor's returns will continue to increase his or her capital, allowing for financial freedom that was not possible with the old day job. From there, it is up to the individual to use that financial autonomy however he or she sees fit.

This is what gets many people interested in binary options trading. Unfortunately, it also sometimes serves as a catalyst for the draining of funds by an overly hopeful investor. However, if the investor is cautious with his or her capital and realistic regarding the chances of a high win rate using binary options trading, this should not be a problem. When applied sensibly, the dream of monetary freedom can be the motivation needed to continue trading even after periods of loss and propel the trader into binary options trading success.

Chapter 17 - Mistakes to Avoid

While becoming a successful options trader isn't possible without making mistakes and learning from them. There are plenty of serious pitfalls that you can be aware of in such a way that it makes you less likely to have to experience them yourself. Keep the following in mind and remember, forewarned is forearmed.

Chasing bottoms and tops: There are certainly some strategies out there that are effective when used near the turning points of existing trends. These are in the minority, however, which means that picking bottoms and tops is, more often than not, a risky proposition. Unfortunately, it is an all too common mistake for traders to invest money into securities that are either too low or too high, gleefully ignoring the 2 percent rule as they do so. This impulse should be avoided like the plague and replaced with a focus on major inbound price moves instead. Sticking to one side of markets that are range-bound will lead to better long-term results at least 90 percent of the time.

Letting your losses build: In order to be truly successful, it is important to make a concentrated effort to keep your expectations for a trade and the reality of the trade separate. The fact of the matter is that once a trade enters losing territory it is unlikely to rebound enough that it actually makes a decent profit and as such, they find that it is best to nip losses in the bud as early as possible. New traders often make the mistake of sticking with certain trades, even after signs begin pointing to a loss because they take trading personally, possibly because they think a failed trade is a reflection on them, or because they simply don't like to lose. Regardless of the reasons behind it, doubling down on a losing trade is only ever asking for trouble.

Like simply sticking with a losing trading, many new traders are also fond of buying in at an additional amount for a losing trade in yet another effort to turn things around. While this type of strategy can work for those who are investing, trying this while trading is akin to flushing your money down the drain. Adding to a losing position is like trying to dig yourself out of a hole, it is never going to work no matter how hard you try.

This is why it is so important to get comfortable setting stop losses that align with the level of risk that you are willing to take with the stock you are currently trading. While it is always possible that a stop loss could trigger due to the natural ebb and flow of price, the simple fact that they are guaranteed to prevent you from dealing with staggering losses is enough to make them worth the risk. Many new traders go to the trouble of setting a decent stop loss only to cancel it right before it is about to trigger in hopes that things are going to turn around. Treat stop losses as part of your plan and never alter your plan when your emotions are controlling your actions, doing so is only asking for trouble.

Sticking with relative trends: If a trend is already well-defined in the market then it is entirely possible that it is going to continue long enough for you to make some money off of it but it is far from a guarantee. The market will naturally fluctuate up to 20 percent of its current average with very little warning, before settling back to the current standard. This means that if you recklessly jump onto a specific trend without doing the required homework you will frequently find yourself making a momentum play that is never going to go anywhere.

Before you make a move regarding a specific trend, there are three distinct timeframes you are going to want to consider first. If you are prone to trading in the short-term then you are going to want to keep an eye on the weekly hourly and daily charts. If you prefer holding onto trades for a longer period of time then daily, weekly and monthly charts are typically going to be more useful.

Trying to fit a square peg into a round hole: There are a myriad of different trading strategies out there and finding the right one for you means first understanding that every trader is different, they have varying goals, varying timeframes in which to achieve their goals and also varying levels of risk that they consider acceptable. As such, the first thing that you are going to need to do is to figure out what your personal investment strategy is going to look like. For some folks, it will involve doing everything they can in order to ensure their principle doesn't decrease, while others are going to feel comfortable risking it all for the promise of an even greater reward.

Depending on the goals you have, you may even be better off creating several different long-term investments, with each being tied to a different specific goal. Regardless, you are also going to need to ensure that you clearly understand why it is you are doing what you are doing and how it is going to help you reach your desired results. When making your plan, it is also important that you realize that it is not going to take place in a vacuum which means you are going to want to create a timeframe that factors in external time sinks along with anything and everything else that is likely to prevent you from reaching your goals. This is a crucial step in order to ensure that your plan is based in reality and is not simply some flight of fancy.

In order to ensure that your goals are achievable, it is important to consider how you feel about risk which can be done by simply asking yourself the question how much money would you be comfortable losing. When determining this amount, it is important to remember that no investment is completely without risk, no matter how much of a sure thing it may seem like on the surface. While this can be scary to think about, it is actually a good thing in the end as without risk there would be no profit.

When it comes to your overall willingness to bet it all for the promise of big rewards, this will be partially due to your innate nature and partially the amount of time you have available to work with your investments prior to reaching your desired goal. For example, if you are still 20 years or more from retirement then you can likely take much greater risks as you have more time for things to balance out than, say, someone who is about to retire next year.

Averaging down: Most traders tend to wander across averaging down. It isn't what they had in mind when they first start to trade but end up doing so anyway. Several problems can arise when averaging down. The main thing is that they can lose a position that they are holding on to. This is sacrificing money and time. This money and time could be placed elsewhere that could prove itself to be better.

If you look at the lost capital, you will need a larger capital on the capital that remains in order to get it back. If a trader were to lose half of their capital, it is going to take a one hundred percent return to get them back to their beginning capital. Losing huge amounts of money with one trade or even in one day can harm their capital for a long time. Even if it works some of the time, averaging down could end up causing a large loss or a margin call, since trends are able to sustain itself for a longer time than a trader is able to stay liquid. This will hold true if you add in more capital and positions start to move away from money.

No one likes losses, but taking small ones is better than getting into a position that could cost you the entire game. There is going to be more trading opportunities if you can learn to save capital. Find a trading plan and stick to it.

Struggling to get even: If you ever hope to be an expert trader, you need to get used to the idea of being wrong regularly and then work it into your business plan. Letting emotion come into play when you make the wrong bet will only lead you to make additional mistakes down the line. The goal should always be to focus on the cold logic behind the numbers, not a hunt for a way to improve your personal image or self-esteem. Always focus on price action, leave the worry about magic numbers and breaking even for when trading is done for the day. The final win/loss ratio can't be tallied until the last trade is made.

Under or overstaying your welcome: Many traders find that they have a good entry plan but a poor exit strategy. This, in turn, leads them to choose a less than ideal time to exit a given trade which leaves them stuck with an investment when they were only looking for a trade. If you find yourself in this scenario it is important to add detailed technical specifications that will determine when you will exit the trade in question. The specifics of this maneuver will likely change over time and it is common for the strategy to evolve over years, not weeks or months.

Gambling: While there is an inherent level of risk in every trade, there is a wide disparity between that and actual gambling. When trading your goal should always be to capitalize on predictive directional signals you have gleaned from checking the statistic, never to bet your money on a hunch. Your goal should be to ensure you remain as disciplined when it comes to making trades as possible. If you are interested in gambling with the stock market, you will likely find better odds for a return on investment in Las Vegas.

Conclusion

Let's hope it was informative and able to provide you with all of the tools you need to achieve your goals whatever they may be.

The next step is to first try trading options on paper. This way, you will be able to visualize actual trades without losing any money. Try and build your confidence this way and then move to an online trade simulator. Here, you will trade just like you would on a broker's platform. However, you will use virtual money.

It is only after you are thoroughly versed with options trading, including common terminology, trading strategies, and so on that, you can now sign up with a broker and open a trading account. If you follow the instructions in this book, then you will begin making good profits in no time. Options are very lucrative and can make you wealthy if applied well.

I want to take a moment before we part ways to celebrate you for investing the time in learning how to conduct trades. Trading can be an intimidating topic, but as you may notice by now it is certainly not challenging to engage in once you know what you are doing. Although the stakes may seem higher because they involve cash money, the general consensus remains the same: as long as you continue to educate yourself on how to make this strategy work and you continue honing your skills, it will become easier.

You absolutely have what it takes to be an excellent trader and to earn massive income through day trading stocks. Simply take your time getting started, educate yourself on each step as you go, build your confidence, and manage your mindset around your trades and you will be generating massive income in no time. The more you invest in building your confidence and your skill, the better you are going to become as a trader. Remember, you always want to strive for improvements even if you think you are already good enough as this is how you prevent yourself from becoming complacent. As long as you stay alert and focused, you will certainly become successful.

www.ingramcontent.com/pod-product-compliance
Lightning Source LLC
Chambersburg PA
CBHW070352220526
45467CB00001B/342